the guide to rer

homeopathy
essential oils
crystals
home remedies

METRO BOOKS
NEW YORK

Designed and created with the Bridgewater Book Company Ltd.

Metro Books
122 Fifth Avenue
New York, NY 10011

ISBN-13: 978-0-7607-5441-2
ISBN-10: 0-7607-5441-1

Printed and bound in Indonesia

5 7 9 10 8 6

NOTE
Any information given in this book is not intended to be taken as a replacement for medical advice. Any person with a condition requiring medical attention should consult a qualified medical practitioner or therapist before taking any of the remedies described in this book.

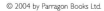

contents

Introduction   **4**

Homeopathy   **6**

Essential oils   **68**

Crystals   **130**

Home remedies   **192**

Index   **254**

Introduction

Today, many of us are interested in finding alternative ways of staying healthy that do not rely on conventional medicine. This book offers a collection of traditional, natural remedies that can be used to treat everyday complaints without the need to turn to the modern medicine cabinet. The remedies suggested here are suitable for young and old alike. They can be used to ease specific symptoms or to enhance general well-being.

The first section deals with homeopathy, which can be used to self-treat many common ailments, as well as to complement conventional medicine. Homeopathy considers every aspect of a person—physical, emotional, and mental—before a treatment is proposed. Two people with the same symptoms will not necessarily be prescribed the same remedy. Homeopathy is based on the principle of treating like with like. Medicines are made from flowers, plants, roots, trees, poisons, minerals, metals, and even from certain insects. The current popularity of homeopathy means that qualified practitioners are easy to find and that remedies are widely available.

The use of essential oils is an accessible form of complementary treatment which has also become more widespread. It is a well-known fact that scents and aromas can affect our mood, helping us to relax or lifting our spirits. Aromatherapy takes this idea one step

Traditional remedies are made from natural sources such as flowers, plants, roots, minerals, and metals.

further, using particular oils to treat specific conditions, either by inhaling them, or by applying them to the skin. Essential oils produced from roots, wood, resins, leaves, berries, seeds, and fruit can have gentle, nurturing effects on body and mind.

The beautiful, natural minerals we call crystals can be used not only to enhance our environment, but also as powerful healing tools. This section links 32 precious stones to their different colors. It looks at their geology and history and teaches us how to share the positive energies of their light, color and beauty. The role of crystals in balancing the chakras (the body's seven energy centers) is also explained.

Finally, we turn to the kitchen for traditional home remedies that date back many years. No longer dismissed as old wives' tales, the treatments in this section are effective for first-aid uses as well as for many general ailments. Everyday natural ingredients can be used in all kinds of forms such as poultices, drinks, or rubs for immediate relief, or added to your diet for long-term benefit. From healing burns, bites, and bruises to soothing arthritis, eczema, and even hangovers, home remedies have the answer.

The scents and aromas of natural oils heal, soothe, and nurture the body and mind.

Serious medical conditions should always be treated by a professional and the information given in this book is not intended to replace the advice of your doctor. Nevertheless, any of the four branches of complementary remedies explored here can lead you toward an understanding of how to heal yourself, while offering an excellent source of front-line treatment.

homeopathy

Introduction

Homeopathy is one of many alternative and complementary therapies available today. Such therapies take a holistic approach to the treatment of patients. The word "holistic" is taken from the Greek word "holos" meaning "whole." The idea is that the person is treated as a whole, with every aspect of them—physical, emotional, and mental—being taken into account when selecting a remedy.

The purpose of this section is to introduce and describe the effects of the most common homeopathic remedies, enabling the reader to choose a remedy for the

Your doctor can refer you to a trained homeopath or another medical doctor who uses homeopathic treatments.

self-treatment of many common ailments, or to use them to complement conventional treatment. It should be stressed, however, that using this book for self-treatment should not replace conventional medicine. If you are concerned about your health, you should visit your doctor for a diagnosis before prescribing yourself any of the remedies. If you are currently under medical supervision, or are on a prescribed course of treatment, then check with your doctor or consultant before self-treating.

Although this book is a good way to begin self-treatment with homeopathy, it is worth noting that other forms of homeopathic treatment are also available.

Some hospitals offer homeopathic treatments from medically qualified doctors. Talk to your personal physician for referral. There are also medical doctors who are trained in homeopathy who work from their own practices, as well as non-medically qualified homeopaths who work in the same way. Some health care providers offer cover for homeopathic referral and treatment; check what is offered by your company.

Homeopathy has grown in popularity in recent years, and main street pharmacies now sell a large selection of homeopathic medicines. Some pharmacists are also trained in homeopathic pharmacy, so they may be able

Today, homeopathic remedies are widely available. Many main street pharmacies stock a range of homeopathic medicines.

to help you choose a remedy. General stores, health food stores, airports, mail order, and internet companies also stock many of the most common remedies, so your chosen remedy should be easy to obtain.

Minor ailments such as colds can be successfully treated using homeopathy at home.

What is Homeopathy?

Homeopathy uses dilute substances to stimulate the body's healing power. Its basic principle is treat "like with like." This involves treating a patient's symptoms with minute amounts of a substance that would cause similar symptoms in a healthy person. This practice contrasts with conventional allopathic medicine, where treating "like with opposite" prevails; that is, a disease is treated with a substance that opposes it.

The first person to practice the healing principle of treating "like with like" was Greek physician Hippocrates (c.460–377BCE). His method went against the thinking of the time, which held that the gods were the main force behind a disease, and that a cure could be found by treating with a substance that had an opposite effect in a healthy person.

German doctor Samuel Hahnemann (1755–1843) was the modern-day founder of homeopathy. He proved the principle of "like curing like" with his experiments with quinine, known to be an effective treatment for malaria. He found he developed malarial symptoms after taking doses of quinine (he was otherwise in good health). These effects lasted hours after each dose.

Samuel Hahnemann devised the system of homeopathy.

He tested other substances in the same way, in a process known as "proving." He "proved" more than 100 homeopathic remedies in his lifetime, publishing his findings in "The Organon of Rational Medicine" in 1811. He believed that the remedies worked by activating a person's "vital force," that is, the body's own healing potential. Having conducted tests on many volunteers, he came to realize the importance of taking into account the personality traits of each person receiving the treatment. He found that particular "types" of people manifested different symptoms to the same disease and so required treatment with different remedies in accordance with their "type."

American doctor James Tyler Kent (1849–1943) furthered Hahnemann's work on the different "types" of people and the matching of a remedy to their emotional and physical characteristics. These "types" became known as "constitutional types."

Remedy Dilution and Potentization

The mother tincture is prepared from the source material.

One drop of the tincture is diluted with 99 drops of alcohol and water.

The remedy is then succussed. This makes the 1c potency.

Using the 1c potency, the process is then repeated to reach the required potency.

A few drops are added to lactose tablets.

Homeopathic remedies

Remedies can be made from many different substances. The most common sources are flowers, plants, roots, trees, poisons, minerals, and metals. Certain insects are also used.

Hahnemann used the smallest possible amount of a substance to trigger a healing effect. This was to minimize side effects. He realized that the more a substance was diluted, the better the results, provided it was also vigorously shaken (in a process known as succussion) at each stage of dilution. Counter-intuitive though it seems, the less of the original substance that remained in the remedy, the greater its potency and effectiveness.

The process of diluting a remedy to render it effective is called potentization. First an alcohol/water extract is made from the substance. This is the mother tincture. The extract is diluted to the required potency. The main potencies are denoted by x, c, and m: x means the remedy has been diluted one part

mother tincture in 9 drops of water; c means one part of mother tincture in 99 drops of water; and m means one part of mother tincture in 999 drops of water. A 1c potency is one part in 99 parts of water. A 2c potency is created by taking one part of the previous dilution (i.e., the 1c potency) and diluting it in 99 parts of water. The most common potencies used are 6c, 12c, and 30c.

Once the required potency is reached, a few drops of the substance are applied to lactose (milk sugar) tablets. The tablets must be kept dry and away from direct sunlight.

For the purposes of self-treatment as detailed here, it is suggested that the 30c potencies are used, as these are commonly available. To obtain the best results, consult a homeopath. They may prescribe higher potencies depending on the initial consultation and the presenting problem. This is particularly the case if the ailment has a strong emotional or mental aspect.

Using the Remedies

When taking the remedies orally it is possible to choose from several mediums that are available from a homeopathic pharmacy or supplier. The tablets also can often be found in a main street pharmacy or health store.

Tablets

These are the most readily available form. The tablets should be sucked or lightly chewed until they dissolve completely. This usually takes several minutes. Tablets are ideal for adults and older children.

Soft Tablets

These dissolve instantly on the tongue. They are ideal for young children, babies, and for adults who are impatient and do not want to spend time sucking or chewing.

Pillules

These are small, round, hard pills. They can take longer to dissolve in the mouth than regular tablets. This form is often found in homeopathic first-aid kits because they are smaller than the tablets and fit easily into a smaller container.

Pillules are small tablets that are dissolved slowly in the mouth. They are useful for homeopathic first-aid kits.

Powders

Powders are usually prescribed by homeopaths for a single dose or several-dose treatment of a higher potency remedy (e.g. 200c or over, or 1m and over). They are supplied wrapped in paper and, like soft tablets, dissolve instantly on the tongue. It is possible simply to crush a tablet to make a powder by folding it in paper and hitting it with the back of a metal spoon. The powder can then be held in the paper, made into a funnel shape, and poured into the mouth

Tablets are the most readily available form of homeopathic remedies.

Back pain is a chronic condition that can be treated by taking several tablets a day.

for quick absorption. This method can be used in a first-aid situation to administer a dose to young children or babies, or to children who refuse to take the tablets.

Frequency of Treatment

Once you have chosen a remedy, the next consideration is how often to take it. The main distinction is between acute and chronic conditions (acute illnesses have a rapid onset and short duration, whereas chronic conditions are of long duration and often gradual onset). For an acute condition such as an injury or a stomach upset, take one tablet every one to two hours for the first six doses (you can take fewer if the condition is relieved before this). If the condition does not improve

after six doses, continue with one tablet two or three times a day until the symptoms are relieved. Once there is improvement, stop taking the remedy immediately.

If the condition is chronic, such as irritable bowel syndrome, chronic fatigue syndrome, arthritis, or depression, then one tablet should be taken twice a day until the condition has improved. Once the condition is relieved, stop the treatment immediately.

Stopping the treatment as soon as the condition improves may seem strange, because conventional medicines, such as antibiotics, often require the whole course to be completed. However, in homeopathy, it is of no benefit to continue a treatment once the condition improves.

If you notice no improvement from a remedy after giving it sufficient time to work, or notice only a very minor improvement, it is worth trying another remedy. Always take into account your constitutional type, if possible. The selection of remedies often involves some trial and error.

A bad cold is an acute condition that can be treated by taking a tablet every 1–2 hours.

Constitutional Types

Homeopathy treats the individual as a whole, taking into account physical, emotional, and mental states as well as disease or ailment. Knowing a person's constitutional type offers insight into the best remedy for them. This is particularly important, because two people suffering from the same problem may have different symptoms. They may find that different modalities (influences) improve or worsen their condition. Therefore, they may need to be treated with different remedies, despite having the same illness.

Mental and emotional factors of constitutional types are taken into consideration when prescribing. These include such matters as the individual's fears and anxieties—for example, whether they have a fear of animals, spiders, the dark, thunderstorms, loneliness, robbery, attack, failure, death, or poisoning. It also takes into account an individual's temperament—whether they tend to be tearful, happy, sad, confident, lazy, perfectionist, mild, gentle, caring, optimistic, irritable, aggressive, or spiteful. Then we need to examine whether certain factors affect the

Knowing a person's constitutional type can provide a valuable insight into their problem.

Knowing a person's fears and anxieties helps to reveal the emotional and mental state of the individual.

individual and whether they have an effect on the condition itself. For example, how do they respond to noise? Does music bring on emotional reactions? Are they bright and alert in the morning or dull and unresponsive? Do they like their own company or prefer to be with others? Do they prefer hot or cold weather? Do they prefer dry or wet atmospheres? Do they talk to others about problems or keep themselves to themselves? Do they have strong likes and dislikes for food and drinks?

Physical factors are also important. These aspects include whether the patient is tall or short; fat or thin; long-limbed; under or overweight. Do they have dark rings under the eyes? What is their hair and eye color? Do they have thick, curly, or thin hair? What is their skin texture? Preferred type of clothing? Is their manner of dress formal or casual? Do they have frown lines?

Once you have discerned someone's constitutional type, it is easier to select the most appropriate remedy. For example, consider a person who is suffering from a sore throat and cold. The best remedy for the physical symptoms of a sore throat and cold is remedy A, B, or C. The best remedy for the emotional aspects of the person with the sore throat and cold is either remedy B or C. The best remedy according to the person's constitution is remedy B. Therefore, remedy B is likely to be most effective.

It is not essential to calculate the remedy in this way—prescribing remedy A based on the physical symptoms only will have some effect— but the best effect would be remedy B, because it fits all aspects for that individual.

Some of the main constitutional types are outlined on the next few pages.

The Argent. Nit. Type

Appearance: Pale complexion. Looks older than actual age, due to worry and tension.

Mental and emotional aspects: Cheerful and impressionable. Often anxious and worried. Always in a hurry and can be impulsive. Finds it difficult to control emotions. Readily laughs, cries, and loses temper. Quick-thinking and good at solving problems. Tends to be extroverted in order to hide true feelings.

Physical weaknesses: Nervous system. Digestive system. Eyes. Ailments tend to be left-sided.

Dietary factors: Likes chocolates, candies, salt, and cheese. Dislikes chilled foods.

The Argent. nit. child: Always moving around and never wants to sit still. Prone to nervousness and can experience upset stomach when stressed. May react badly to new situations such as moving school. Can be prone to insomnia due to anxiety. Prone to bedwetting.

Argent. nit. types tend to have weak mucous membranes in their eyes.

The Arsen. Alb. Type

Appearance: Usually thin or slim. Often well groomed and "stylish." Fine facial features with delicate, sensitive skin. Frown lines can appear on the forehead.

Mental and emotional aspects: Restless person. Perfectionist at work and at home. Can be critical and intolerant. Strong opinions. Can have a deep fear of being alone. Obsessive-compulsive behavior, in particular involving cleanliness and "tidying up"; this can hide a hoarding mentality. Can pull out of plans and projects early if they think it is not going to work out 100%.

Warm drinks and sweet foods are favored by the Arsen. alb. type.

Pessimistic in nature, with a need to receive constant reassurance.

Physical weakness: Digestive system. Skin. Respiratory system (asthma, coughs, and colds).

Dietary factors: Likes fatty foods, warm food and drinks, in particular coffee, candies, alcohol, and sour-tasting foods. Dislikes large amount of fluid.

The Arsen. alb. child: Highly sensitive and "highly strung." Easily upset by loud noise. Becomes tired and exhausted after periods of exertion. Suffers nightmares due to very active imagination. Increasingly physically and mentally agile with age. Can worry too much about parents' well-being. Keeps room neat and tidy. Does not like mess or getting messy.

The Calc. Carb. Type

Appearance: Overweight or gains weight easily. Sluggish, bloated, and tired in appearance. May have poor posture.

Mental and emotional aspects: Impressionable. Sensitive and quiet. May become withdrawn due to a deep fear of failure. Can dwell too much on a particular problem. May be greatly upset by cruelty to animals or children. Needs motivation to succeed in tasks. Can be prone to mild depression when unwell. Reassurance helps to improve condition.

Physical weaknesses: Ears, nose, and throat. Skeletal system (may manifest in backache). Digestive system: may be prone to irritable bowel syndrome and bloatedness. Skin. Teeth. Exhaustion; prone to chronic fatigue syndrome. Prone to depression.

Dietary factors: Likes dairy products, eggs, candies, salt, desserts, chocolate, carbohydrates, iced drinks, and ice-cream. Dislikes fatty meat, boiled food, and boiled milk.

The Calc. carb. child: Plump and overweight. Placid and calm. Complexion often pale. Slow to walk and talk and teeth are slow to develop. Can fall over easily. Scared of the dark and prone to waking up because of nightmares. Often lazy and may need encouragement with schoolwork as gives up easily.

The ears, nose, and throat are all weak areas of the Calc. carb. type.

The Graphites Type

Appearance: Prone to being overweight and has a large appetite. Blushes easily. Can have a rugged, windswept appearance. May have rough, dry skin that can crack and flake easily. Dry hair, usually dark in color. Flaky scalp.

Mental and emotional aspects: A plodder—takes time to work things out and solve problems. Deep concentration on a task can cause irritability. Unwilling to change attitudes and routines. Not best first thing in the morning. Prone to mood swings. Can become tearful and despondent and then impatient.

Physical weaknesses: Skin. Nails. Slow metabolic rate. Common ailments may include soreness in the corners of the mouth, exhaustion, bad breath, nose bleeds, styes, and travel sickness.

Dietary factors: Likes sour and savory foods, cool drinks. Dislikes sweet foods, salt, seafood, hot drinks.

The Graphites child: Feels the cold and gets chilled very quickly. Timid, hesitant, and anxious. Does not like long periods of travel, as often suffers from travel sickness.

The Graphites type likes savory foods, such as salads or vegetables, rather than candies and desserts.

The Ignatia Type

Appearance: Slim build. Prone to dark circles under the eyes. May have a tired, drawn expression and involuntary twitching of the eyes and mouth. Dry lips. Hair is of a dark to medium color. Sighs a lot.

Mental and emotional aspects: The most highly strung of the constitutional types. Tendency to rapid and extreme mood swings. Can switch quickly from depression to joy and from tears to laughter. Prone to suppressing grief. May find it difficult to end relationships and perceive this to be a weakness. Addictions to nicotine and caffeine are common.

Physical weaknesses: Nervous system. Emotional trauma may be the cause of any number of physical problems. Common problems include hysterical grief over bereavement, leading to depression, headaches, sore throats, coughs and colds, constipation, twitching, and grinding of teeth.

Dietary factors: Likes coffee (although it may not agree with them), sour and savory foods, dairy products, carbohydrates. Dislikes sweet foods.

The Ignatia child: Highly strung. Excitable and sensitive. Finds it difficult to perform under stress. Finds separation or divorce of parents very hard to deal with, leading to outbursts of anger, crying, and poor performance at school. Prefers company to being alone. May suffer with headaches, coughs, sore throats. Responds well to reassurance.

Dairy foods are popular with the Ignatia type.

The Lachesis Type

Appearance: May look bloated or lean. Strong, fixed expression. Complexion usually pale and prone to slight freckles. Strong and staring eyes. Can lick the lips a lot.

Mental and emotional aspects: Very ambitious. Highly creative. Mind can become crowded with thoughts. Jealous and possessive. Talkative. Can be sensitive to noise. If religious, is prone to view self as sinful. Can be suspicious of strangers.

Physical weaknesses: Circulation. Nervous system. Common problems include varicose veins, hyperactivity, menopausal problems, sore throats, and asthma, disturbed sleep and insomnia, palpitations, and panic attacks. Prone to left-sided problems. Physical problems made worse when trying to sleep or remain still.

Dietary factors: Likes coffee, alcohol, seafood, cool drinks, sour and savory food, and carbohydrates. Dislikes sweet drinks.

The Lachesis child: Spiteful, possessive, and can be hurtful to peers. Hyperactive. Jealous of siblings, particularly newly born. Prone to nightmares. May be prone to ADHD (attention deficit and hyperactivity disorder).

Lachesis types have a tendency to lick their top lip.

The Lycopodium Type

Appearance: Tall and lean. Worry and frown lines on the forehead. Can look older than their actual years. Facial twitches. Thinning hair in men. Dislikes wearing tight clothing.

Mental and emotional aspects: Prone to exaggeration. Can create a drama over minor matters. Insecure and hates change. Avoids commitment. Anxious of challenging events. Strong fear of being alone and of the dark. Forgetful. Finds small mistakes disproportionately irritating. Hates being contradicted.

Physical weakness: Common problems include digestive disorders, kidney stones, prostate problems, headaches, sore throats, male-pattern baldness, and alopecia. May be prone to chronic fatigue syndrome.

Right-sided problems are more prevalent.

Dietary factors: Likes sweet foods, warm drinks, onions, garlic, and seafood. Dislikes cheese and strongly flavored meats.

The Lycopodium child:
Basically insecure and shy, although can be bossy and dominant with other children. Likes to be indoors rather than doing outdoor pursuits. Likes to read and is conscientious and good academically.

The hairline of Lycopodium men recedes early and they may become prematurely gray or bald.

The Merc. Sol. Type

Appearance: Medium build. Skin on the face may be shiny or moist due to perspiration, with a gray translucent look. Hair color may be fair to medium.

Mental and emotional aspects: May have an inner battle with emotions. Resentment, anxiety, and lack of trust in others may cause feelings of insecurity. Dislikes criticism that is directed at self or taking orders from others. May explode with rage and anger.

Memory may become poor with age and thought patterns may become muddled later in life.

Physical weaknesses: Common problems include sore throat; swelling of glands; exhaustion. Skin sensitivity and allergies are common. May be prone to chronic fatigue syndrome. May suffer from SAD (seasonal affective disorder).

Dietary factors: Likes cold drinks, carbohydrates, and citrus fruits. Dislikes strongly flavored foods.

The Merc. sol. child: Irritating behavior. Shy and cautious. May have a tendency to stammer. Susceptible to ear, nose, and throat ailments.

The Merc. sol. type may be affected by changes in the weather or may suffer from SAD (seasonal affective disorder).

The Nat. mur. type

Appearance: Pear-shaped build in women. Solid, strong-to-lean build in men. Skin can be oily and puffy with a tendency to swell. Red, watery eyes. Dry cracked lips. Medium to dark hair.

Mental and emotional aspects: Prone to suppressing emotions such as fear, loneliness, guilt, and anger, which can lead to depression. Suppressed feelings of grief or loss for a loved one or. for the self. Can become very despondent and depressed after relationship break-up. May want to cry but cannot. Prone to suffer in silence and not ask for help when needed. Career-minded and successful with a serious outlook on life.

Physical weaknesses: Nervous system. Common problems include: depression; premenstrual

syndrome; anorexia; skin problems; mouth ulcers and cold sores; palpitations and headaches.

Dietary factors: Likes cool drinks, sour and savory foods and craves salt and most carbohydrates. Dislikes coffee and bread.

The Nat. mur. child: Small for their age. Slow development. Well-behaved. Loves animals. Excellent academically but if criticized at school can become very hurt. Can be prone to headaches under pressure.

Nat. mur. types are serious and conscientious. They may be professional and career-minded.

The Nux Vomica Type

Appearance: Slim, particularly when young. Smart appearance. May look stressed and tense. Ages prematurely. Prone to dark circles under the eyes. Face becomes flushed through anger or excitement.

Mental and emotional aspects: Can suffer from addictions and over-indulgence. May have cravings for alcohol, food, and stimulants such as coffee and cigarettes. Can be addicted to sex. Finds it difficult to relax. Can be very ambitious. Impatient. Intolerant

The Nux vomica type may become overdependent on alcohol or stimulants, which may be craved.

and critical and requires perfection in others. The worst thing that can happen to a Nux vomica type is failure.

Physical weaknesses: Digestive disorders from hangovers and overindulgence. Migraines and headaches, hernia, and hay fever. Feels better for sleep.

Dietary factors: Likes fatty and rich food, cheese and cream, alcohol, coffee and spicy foods. Dislikes the effect of some strong spicy foods (despite enjoying eating them).

The Nux vomica child: Irritable and easily bored. May be prone to hyperactivity and ADHD (attention deficit and hyperactivity disorder). May throw tantrums. Competitive as a teenager. Can become addicted to alcohol and drugs, as likes to be rebellious.

The Phosphorus Type

Appearance: Tall and slim with long limbs. Likes to dress well and look stylish. May be artistic and creative in appearance. Fine skin. Can have fair to dark hair.

Mental and emotional aspects: Needs a lot of love and attention. Good fun to be with but can be needy and demanding. Likes to be the center of attraction. Enjoys sympathy when upset or unwell. Expressive, affectionate, and shows emotions easily. Needs reassurance, in particular with looks and body image. Short attention span. Challenging, particularly toward a partner.

Physical weaknesses: Nervous system—in particular fear and hypersensitivity. Circulation

problems. Vertigo. Coughs and colds. Weakness of the lungs. Headaches. Prone to left-sided problems.

Dietary factors: Likes salt, spicy food, sour and savory food, carbonated drinks, alcohol, mild cheeses, and sweet foods. Dislikes strongly flavored fish and fruit.

The Phosphorus child: Tall and slim with long legs and arms. Nervous. Likes to be with people and center of attention. Loves to receive affection. Strong fear of the dark.

Phosphorus types enjoy mild cheeses. They also enjoy spicy, sour, and savory dishes.

The Pulsatilla Type

Appearance: Can be slightly overweight. Gentle and kind in appearance. Can look younger than actual age. Hair is fair and skin has a rosy complexion. Usually has blue eyes. Blushes easily. Often rests with hands behind the head.

Mental and emotional aspects: Shy and easily embarrassed. Kind and gentle and makes friends easily. Likes to be supported by others. Not assertive and can be indecisive. Cries easily, in particular over cruelty to children and animals, tragic news, or weepy movies. Also laughs easily. Avoids confrontation. Loves animals.

Pulsatilla types often rest with their hands behind their head.

Can suppress guilt and anger. Occasionally prone to obsessive or compulsive behavior.

Physical weaknesses: All female reproductive problems. Catarrh. Irritable bowel syndrome. Skin problems. Varicose veins. Styes. Physical symptoms can fluctuate and change rapidly.

Dietary factors: Likes sweet foods, cold foods, and cool drinks. Dislikes fatty foods (particularly cream and butter) and very rich, spicy food.

The Pulsatilla child: Fears the dark and dislikes bedtime. Sensitive to changes in the weather. Becomes tearful and weepy when overtired. Prone to coughs and colds.

The Sepia Type

Appearance: Slim and tall. Often sits with legs crossed. Likes to look attractive and elegant. Medium to dark hair, often with brown eyes.

Mental and emotional aspects: Can be irritable and easily offended. Tendency to be aggressive to loved ones. Cannot handle too much stress and tries to escape pressure and deadlines. Can feel better after weeping, but dislikes it when other people are fussing around. Avoids crowds but fears being alone. Hates being contradicted; holds strong opinions.

Physical weaknesses: These include all menopausal problems. Headaches and migraine. Skin problems. Other common ailments include constipation and hemorrhoids; chronic fatigue syndrome and depression. Conditions usually improve with exertion. Physical problems occur mostly on left side.

Dietary factors: Likes spices, sour and savory food, citrus fruits, sweet foods, and alcohol. Dislikes dairy products, in particular milk, rich and strongly flavored meats, and fatty foods.

The Sepia child: Greedy. Prone to constipation. Can become a bedwetter. Moody. Feels the cold and becomes tired easily. Does not like being alone.

The Sepia type fears being alone but at the same time does not like to be part of a large crowd.

The Silicea Type

Appearance: Often slim or thin, with a large forehead. The head can appear too large for the body. Delicate, fine features—almost doll-like in appearance. The skin of the lips looks gray and can be cracked. The palms of the hand feel sweaty to touch and the nails can be brittle.

Mental and emotional aspects: Appears to have low confidence from a young age. Prone to mental exhaustion. Can become overburdened and overwhelmed. Responsibility weighs heavily upon the Silicea type. Can be indecisive about taking on new projects, moves, and new jobs. Fear of failure may manifest itself as workaholism. Fear of failure

The nails of Silicea types may be rough or brittle. If injured, their skin can take a long time to heal.

can also spread into personal relationships. May stubbornly resist advice from loved ones and friends in order to hide true feelings.

Physical weaknesses: Problems with nervous system, in particular burn-out from new ventures. Exhaustion. Slowness in healing and convalescence. Respiratory illnesses and weaknesses including chest infections and low resistance to coughs and colds. Constipation. Skin problems. Headaches. Feels the cold.

Dietary factors: Likes cold food such as salads and raw vegetables. Dislikes meat and dairy products, in particular cheese and milk. Dislikes very hot food.

The Silicea child: Can be smaller than children of a similar age, with a petite appearance, apart from the head, which may look large for the body size. Feels the cold. Not sporty as has little stamina. Can be shy. Usually tidy and well-behaved.

The Sulfur Type

Appearance: May be slim with poor posture. May look untidy. Hair may be coarse, dry. Skin and lips can be prone to redness.

Mental and emotional aspects: Mind can be cluttered. Can be critical. Likes to argue. May lack willpower and self-esteem. Might not complete ideas or projects.

Physical weakness: Prone to: skin and circulation problems; hemorrhoids and constipation; hot, burning feet; body odor.

Dietary factors: Likes sweet foods, fatty foods, and stimulants such as coffee and chocolate. Likes alcohol, spicy foods, savory foods, citrus fruits, salads, and seafood. Dislikes dairy foods, in particular milk and eggs. Dislikes most hot drinks.

The Sulfur child: Untidy looking. Can be hyperactive in the evening. Does not like bathing, showers or washing hands. Has a very healthy appetite.

The Sulfur type enjoys sour foods such as citrus fruits.

Homeopathic Remedies

In the following pages are details of the main remedies: derivation, treatment use, and tips. Before continuing, read about modalities and get to know the dos and don'ts.

Modalities

Modalities are influences that worsen or improve the symptoms of the patient. They are an invaluable guide to narrowing down the choice of a homeopathic remedy. These are the main types of modality:

• **Physical modalities:** include how the patient is affected by movement, position of the body, touch, rest, exertion, noise, and smells.

• **Temperature:** heat, cold, warmth, wind, damp, and the season of the year may affect the individual's symptoms.

• **Time:** symptoms may be more noticeable in the daytime or at night, or in the morning, afternoon, or evening. Symptoms may even change hourly.

• **Diet:** different foods, drinks, stimulants, or alcohol may affect the patient and his or her ailment.

• **Localized modalities:** symptoms may be worse on the left or right side of the body. Left-handed and right-handed people may experience symptoms differently.

Dos

• Leave your mouth free from food and liquid 20–30 minutes each side of taking the remedy.

• Use a homeopathic toothpaste such as calendula, as this will be free from substances that may antidote the remedy.

• Store the remedy in a dark, cool place.

• Check the expiry date before use.

• Keep tablets out of reach of children and pets.

• Store the remedy away from strong-smelling perfumes or essential oils.

Don'ts

• Don't swallow the tablet; suck it till it dissolves.

• Don't drink coffee or smoke while taking treatment.

• Don't eat mints, peppermints, or menthol cough sweets, because this may interfere with the remedy's action. Avoid brushing your teeth with mint or peppermint-flavored toothpaste.

• Don't use the essential oils of camphor, eucalyptus, menthol, peppermint, or rosemary.

• Don't touch the pills directly. Always tap the tablets into the lid, because the sweat from your fingertips or palm may absorb the remedy rather than your mouth.

• Don't apply perfume or aftershave 30 minutes either side of taking the remedy.

A c o n i t e

Aconite is derived from Monkshood, a toxic plant used for centuries to treat infections and also to poison arrows for hunting.

Treatment Use

Aconite is useful when any of the following are indicated:

Mental and emotional aspects

● Anxiety and great fear ● Feelings of doom and gloom, especially when accompanied by illness ● A strong fear of death, the dark, and ghosts ● Agoraphobia and panic ● Any form of shock ● Worry and stress about the future ● Nightmares ● Panic attacks ● Vivid imagination ● Unhappiness ● Emotional and physical tension that drains energy from the mind and the body.

Aconite is often used to treat panic attacks. It can also be used when a person is facing any situation that is an ordeal.

The Monkshood plant (Aconitum napellus) is the source of the remedy Aconite.

Physical aspects

● Headaches with a hot and heavy sensation ● Sore, gritty eyes ● Sore nose, throat, or ear problems ● Tightness and pressure around the chest ● Coughs, colds, and influenza ● Sleep problems ● Feelings of restlessness ● Palpitations ● Nervous twitching of the eye ● Sunburn, when accompanied by shaking and fever.

Modalities

● **Better:** for fresh air and warmth.
● **Worse:** in the evening and at night.

Treatment Tips

This remedy is useful for treating ailments that develop suddenly.

This remedy is a useful addition to a homeopathic first-aid kit.

Apis Mel.

Apis mel. is derived from the honeybee—the whole bee is used. Propolis, a resin-type substance secreted by bees to repair damage to hive walls, has been used for centuries as a natural antibiotic.

Treatment Use

Apis mel. is useful when any of the following are indicated:

Mental and emotional aspects

• Poor memory • Feelings of jealousy • Being hard to please • Tearfulness • Apathy and indifference • Constantly complaining and hard to please • Fear of death.

Physical aspects

• Clumsiness • Headaches with a stabbing and stinging pain • Fever with a lack of thirst accompanied by skin that is sensitive to the touch • Itchy, stinging skin • All eye problems that sting and burn • Arthritis when the pain is burning in sensation • Cystitis and other urinary tract infections that cause stinging on passing urine

Apis mel. is often used to help overcome tearfulness.

The remedy from the honeybee provides a range of medicinal substances.

• Insect bites and stings • A constant but spasmodic cough.

Modalities

• **Better:** cool water and a cool room; the application of cold compresses.

• **Worse:** for pressure and touch; heat.

Treatment Tips

Apis mel. is an excellent remedy for treating burning and stinging pain that responds well to being treated with a cool remedy. It is useful for swollen and itchy skin, particularly following insect bites and stings. Useful for any sudden swelling or puffiness of the skin.

This remedy is a useful addition to a homeopathic first-aid kit.

Argent. Nit.

Argent. nit. is derived from silver nitrate (a compound of silver). It is poisonous in large amounts. It has a caustic nature and it was used historically to cauterize wounds.

Treatment Use

Argent. nit. is useful when any of the following are indicated:

Silver nitrate crystals are extracted from the mineral acanthite, the main ore of silver.

Mental and emotional aspects

- Apprehension ● Fearfulness
- Nervousness ● Overactive imagination
- Stage-fright ● Phobias, in particular claustrophobia and fear of spiders and insects
- Feeling stressed and in a hurry ● Fear of giving talks or addressing groups ● Fear of taking examinations.

Physical aspects

- Diarrhea caused by anxiety and tension

● Nightmares ● Tight, sore muscles due to constant body tension ● Headaches caused by concentrating hard ● Flatulence ● Trembling and weakness in muscles and limbs ● Palpitations and tightness in the chest ● Aching, tired eyes ● Irritable bowel syndrome.

Modalities

- **Better:** for cool, fresh air and pressure.
- **Worse:** when highly emotional; for concentration; for warmth.

Treatment Tips

A remedy that helps to relieve apprehension and anxiety. Useful when there is fear of a forthcoming event, for example an examination or an interview. Helps control nerves both before and during the event.

Argent. nit. can be used to help overcome fears and phobias and help with nightmares or an overactive imagination.

Arnica

Arnica is derived from the herb *Arnica montana* (also known as Leopard's Bane, Wolf's Bane, or Mountain Arnica) a plant used since the 16th century as a remedy for bruises, muscular aches and pains, and rheumatism.

The fresh flowers of the plant Arnica montana *are used to provide a remedy for physical and emotional shock.*

- Hot, sensitive, aching headache ● Heavy, tired eyes ● Concussion ● Nosebleeds
- Sore muscles in chest following a bad cough
- Over-exertion ● Vertigo.

Modalities

- **Better:** for lying down.
- **Worse:** for moving; cold, damp weather.

Treatment Use

Arnica is useful when any of the following are indicated:

Mental and emotional aspects

- Irritability ● Nervousness and oversensitivity ● Inability to focus on a task for long ● Forgetfulness and indifference
- Agoraphobia ● All forms of shock
- Bereavement.

Physical aspects

- Post-surgical convalescence ● Labor pains and childbirth ● Sore muscles ● Swelling
- Bruising ● Backache and joint pain
- Sprains ● Black eyes ● Accidents and falls

Treatment Tips

Arnica is a key remedy for all forms of muscular pain and bruising. It is also very useful applied topically to unbroken skin in a cream or ointment form or as a compress using the tincture. Arnica is one of the most commonly used remedies and is an over-the-counter bestseller.

This remedy is a useful addition to a homeopathic first-aid kit.

Arnica is a useful remedy for the physical and emotional impact of childbirth.

Arsen. Alb.

Arsen. alb. is derived from arsenic, which is a metallic poison.

Treatment Use

Arsen. alb is useful when any of the following are indicated:

Mental and emotional aspects

- Restlessness • Anguish and anxiety
- Feelings of hopelessness • Overreaction to ailments • Agitation • Hypochondria
- Perfectionism demonstrated by obsessive-compulsive behavior • Inability to cope
- Insecurity • Fear of the dark • Fear of poisoning • Twitches • Fixed ideas • Jealousy
- Addictions, including those to alcohol and tobacco • Fear of being alone • Fear of death
- Fear of suffocation.

Physical aspects

- Skin, hair, and scalp problems, such as psoriasis and dandruff • Food poisoning
- Vomiting • Exhaustion • Headaches
- Mouth ulcers • Fluid retention • Mild forms of asthma • Sore throat, particularly if swallowing is difficult • Cramp • Disturbed, restless sleep • Angina pain.

The arsenic compound arsenic trioxide is used to treat a variety of symptoms.

Modalities

- **Better:** for warm drinks; heat; movement.
- **Worse:** for cold, wet weather.

Treatment Tips

A very useful remedy for the treatment of digestive problems. It is also excellent for treating anxiety and restlessness. It acts on every organ and tissue of the body.

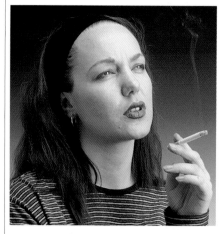

Arsen. alb. acts on the mucous membranes of the digestive tract and respiratory system. It can be used to treat addictions such as smoking.

Aurum Met.

Aurum met. is derived from gold that has first been ground to a powder.

Treatment Use

Aurum met. is useful when any of the following are indicated:

Pure gold ground to a fine powder is used to make Aurum met.

Mental and emotional aspects

● Tendency to become a workaholic ● Prone to perfectionism, leading to dissatisfaction ● Can become deeply upset if criticized ● Extreme unhappiness ● Depression, sometimes leading to suicidal thoughts ● Obsessed with illness and death ● Illness triggered by grief ● Fixed ideas ● Prone to criticize everyone around them ● Cannot always share worries with others, instead brooding on them in isolation ● Prone to nightmares ● Anxiety triggered by loud noises.

Physical aspects

● Illness through depression ● Heart disease, blood and circulatory problems ● Headaches ● Chest pain and breathlessness ● Sinus problems and sinusitis ● Catarrh ● Ear, nose, and throat problems ● Joint pain and skin ulcers ● SAD (seasonal affective disorder).

Modalities

● **Better:** for fresh air and movement.
● **Worse:** for emotional stress and tension; at night; in wintertime.

Treatment Tips

A good remedy to try when others have failed, in particular in cases of depression where there appears to be "no light at the end of the tunnel."

Overwork and stress can be treated by Aurum met. It is used to help many different problems, from depression to heart disease.

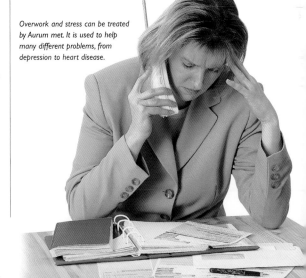

Belladonna

Belladonna is derived from the deadly
nightshade plant, which was popular
during the Middle Ages for magic rituals.

Treatment Use

Belladonna is useful when any of the following
are indicated:

*Although every part of the belladonna plant (Atropa belladonna)
is poisonous, the leaves and flowers are used in homeopathy.*

Mental and emotional aspects

● Sudden anger ● Feelings of guilt ● Stress
● Depression triggered by agitation ● Sudden
temper tantrums and a red face.

Physical aspects

● All pain where there is heat, burning,
redness, or throbbing ● Cold, coughs, and
influenza ● Sore throats ● Earache, made
worse by getting the head wet or cold
● Labor pains ● Cystitis ● All infections that
result in inflammation ● Teething pain ● Boils
● Insomnia.

Modalities

● **Better:** for sitting up.
● **Worse:** for noise and movement.

Treatment Tips

An excellent remedy for acute complaints,
particularly when accompanied by hot,
throbbing sensations.

This remedy is a useful addition
to a homeopathic first-aid kit.

*The remedy Belladonna is used to control sudden anger and violent
outbursts of behavior.*

Bryonia

Bryonia is derived from the roots of wild hops grown in central and southern Europe. Bryonia was used by the Romans to treat coughs and wounds.

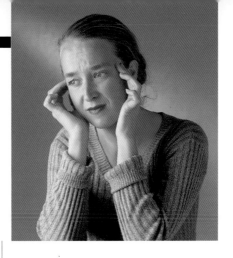

Treatment Use

Bryonia is useful when any of the following are indicated:

Mental and emotional aspects

● Anger, irritability, and restlessness ● Poor memory ● Fear of death ● Prefers to be left alone, particularly when unwell.

Physical aspects

● Headaches with a bursting or splitting sensation ● Arthritis and rheumatism ● Dry eyes and lips ● Very dry and sore throat ● Dry, irritating cough ● Constipation ● Influenza ● Pneumonia ● Pleurisy with severe chest pain ● Colic.

Bryonia is used to treat anger and anxiety, but can also be used as a treatment for violent headaches.

Modalities

● **Better:** for rest and stillness; a cold environment.

● **Worse:** with any kind of movement; cold winds.

Treatment Tips

Best used when there is pain on the slightest movement. Most effective when colds are accompanied by a strong thirst and a very dry throat.

The fresh roots of Bryonia (Bryonia alba) are chopped and pounded to make a pulp for the Bryonia remedy.

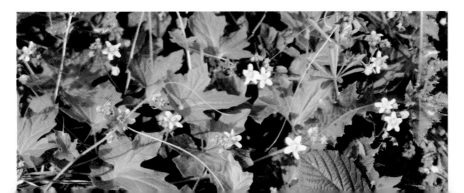

Calc.   Carb.

Calc. carb. is derived from calcium
carbonate in oyster shells.

Treatment Use

Calc. carb. is useful when any of the following
are indicated:

Mental and emotional aspects

- Fear of the dark, death, insanity, and
impending doom ● In the elderly, fear of a
stroke ● Anxiety which can cause palpitations
● Depression with tiredness/lethargy ● Poor
memory ● Tiredness and slowness of thought
● Obsession with problems ● Anxiety when
criticized ● Hypochondria ● Lowness of
spirit● Jealousy ● Laziness ● Fear of disease.

Physical aspects

- Teeth, joint, and bone pain
● Fractures that are slow to
heal ● Back pain ● Digestive
problems ● Irritable bowel

*The mother-of-pearl inside oyster shells contains calcium carbonate.
This salt is ground to a powder to make this remedy.*

syndrome ● Constipation ● Premenstrual
syndrome ● Nasal congestion ● Polyps ● Dry,
irritating, or tickling coughs ● Obesity ● Eating
disorders, in particular bulimia ● Chronic
fatigue syndrome ● Warts ● Headaches
caused by study or when head feels heavy
● Light-sensitive eyes ● Loss of hearing
● Dark rings around the eyes ● Sour taste
in the mouth ● Bleeding gums ● Toothache
● Cramp ● Stiff neck ● Weakness in the
knees ● Unhealthy-looking skin.

*The Calc. carb.
remedy is used to
help with anxiety,
fear, depression,
and feelings
of extreme
helplessness.*

Modalities

- **Better:** for warm weather.
- **Worse:** when cold and damp; for exertion.

Treatment Tips

An excellent remedy for when bones are slow
to heal.

Calc. Phos.

Calc. phos. is derived from the mineral salt calcium phosphate.

Treatment Use

Calc. phos. is useful when any of the following are indicated:

Mental and emotional aspects

- Unhappiness and discontentment with life, possibly stemming from childhood
- Relationship break-ups may trigger the onset of an illness • Prone to irritability
- Can complain a lot • Tendency to become restless • Difficulty keeping to routines
- In constant need of new things for stimulation • Poor memory.

Physical aspects

- Breaks, fractures, and painful joints • Slow bone or tooth growth in children and teenagers • Exhaustion and fatigue
- Digestive disorders
- Recurrent throat problems.

Modalities

- **Better:** for warm, dry, sunny weather.
- **Worse:** in the cold or damp; for stress and worry.

Calc. phos. is made into a powder through a chemical process.

Treatment Tips

A good remedy if healing is slow or for any bone and joint complaints. It can be used to help "growing pains" in children and adolescents. Good for convalescence.

Calcium phosphate occurs naturally in our teeth, making them hard and rigid. The remedy can be used to treat tooth decay.

Cantharis

Cantharis is derived from a bright green beetle known as the Spanish fly, which has been known for centuries for its poisonous and irritant properties.

Treatment Use

Cantharis is useful when any of the following are indicated:

Mental and emotional aspects

● Addiction to sex ● Irritability and anger leading to rage and violence ● Screaming with rage ● Severe anxiety.

Physical aspects

● All conditions where there is stinging, burning, itching, and pain ● Cystitis and all urinary tract infections, with pain when urinating ● Burns ● Diarrhea with burning sensation ● Insect stings and bites ● Burning,

The Spanish fly is the source of the Cantharis remedy.
It secretes a substance called cantharidin, which is an irritant.

sore throat ● Sore, stinging eyes ● Hot, aching sensation in the stomach ● Sunburn and inflammation of the skin.

Modalities

● **Better:** for gentle rubbing.
● **Worse:** for touch and movement.

Treatment Tips

Excellent remedy for treatment of cystitis, especially when the condition worsens without warning.

This remedy is a useful addition to a homeopathic first-aid kit.

The remedy Cantharis can be used to treat ailments that have burning symptoms, including sunburn.

Carbo Veg.

Carbo veg. is derived from vegetable charcoal made from beech, birch, or poplar wood. In the past, vegetable charcoal was used to absorb gases to help relieve flatulence.

Woods from trees such as beech, birch, or poplar are partly burned to make charcoals that have individual properties.

● Indigestion ● Flatulence ● Feelings of abdominal bloating (even after eating only small amounts) ● Headaches after too much food ● Headaches with sickness ● Coughing ● Hoarseness and dryness of the throat ● Nosebleeds ● Prolonged illness, leaving feelings of exhaustion.

Modalities

● **Better:** for cool, fresh air.
● **Worse:** for fatty foods; in the evening; for lying down.

Treatment Use

Carbo veg. is useful when any of the following are indicated:

Mental and emotional aspects

● Loss of memory ● Fear of strangers
● Claustrophobia ● Acute shock ● Extreme mental exhaustion ● Feelings of mental and emotional weakness.

Physical aspects

● Poor circulation ● Varicose veins

Treatment Tips

A very good remedy for feelings of overtiredness and being run down. Useful after any operation or illness. Good for speeding a slow recovery. Good for chronic complaints or conditions.

Carbo veg. is mainly given for exhaustion, weakness, and lack of energy. It is useful to take following an illness.

Chamomilla

Chamomilla is derived from the whole, fresh chamomile plant. Chamomile has been used for centuries because of its calming, soothing, and healing abilities, particularly in the treatment of skin conditions.

Treatment Use

Chamomilla is useful when any of the following are indicated:

Chamomilla is derived from the juices of the whole, fresh plant (Matricaria recutita) in flower.

Mental and emotional aspects

- Bad temper and anger when unwell
- Irritability and whining ● Impatience
- Oversensitivity, which can lead to short-

tempered behavior toward loved ones
- Difficult to satisfy.

Physical aspects

- Earache ● Toothache
- Insomnia ● All skin conditions including eczema ● Inflamed skin
- Sleeplessness and colic in children
- Diarrhea ● Coughing, particularly at night.

Modalities

- **Better:** for mild weather.
- **Worse:** for heat; for cold winds or fresh air; when angry.

Treatment Tips

Especially good remedy for the treatment of children or babies. Chamomilla is a good bedtime remedy for a baby. Teething problems or colic may cause the baby to cry out and be restless. Chamomilla will help the baby to calm down and sleep.

Chamomilla is good for people who suffer from sleeplessness, or who cry out in their sleep because of anxious dreams.

China

China is derived from Peruvian bark, which contains quinine—one of the first remedies investigated by Samuel Hahnemann.

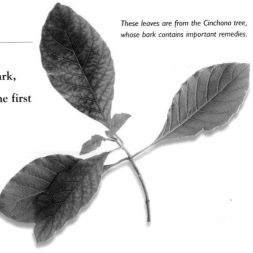

These leaves are from the Cinchona tree, whose bark contains important remedies.

Treatment Use

China is useful when any of the following are indicated:

Mental and emotional aspects

● Indifference and apathy ● Nervous exhaustion ● Despair ● Fear of creeping, crawling creatures ● Outbursts of anger ● Spitefulness ● Sudden tearfulness ● Depression ● Eating disorders such as anorexia and bulimia ● Lack of concentration ● Feelings of being on edge ● Hypersensitivity ● Alcoholism ● Difficulty in self-expression.

Physical aspects

● Loss of body fluid through heat-stroke ● Heavy sweating ● Fluid retention ● Swollen ankles ● Headaches ● Dizziness ● Twitches ● Nosebleeds ● Tinnitus ● Digestive problems including diarrhea and vomiting ● Gall bladder complaints

● Feelings of coldness ● Shivering ● Fatigue, including post-viral exhaustion ● Chronic fatigue syndrome ● Skin that is sensitive to the touch ● Tender scalp.

Modalities

● **Better:** for warmth and sleep.

● **Worse:** for losing bodily fluids; for cold and drafts.

Treatment Tips

A good remedy for burn-out caused by overwork or emotional traumas that produce feelings of exhaustion and weakness. Also a good convalescent remedy.

The China remedy is helpful for irritability and unexpected angry outbursts.

Coffea

Coffea is derived from caffeine:
the unroasted coffee bean is used.

Treatment Use

Coffea is useful when any of the
following are indicated:

Mental and emotional aspects

- Hyperactivity and inability to rest the mind
- Insomnia • Overexcitement in children
- Anxiety and feelings of irritability • Sensory
overload • Feelings of guilt, particularly over
children • Problems in relationships that

*Coffea is used to treat overactive mental activity including
hyperactivity and overexcitement in children.*

*Beans roasted for coffee are derived from ripe berries of the Coffea
arabica tree. The berries are also used for the Coffea remedy.*

cause physical problems such as headaches
and migraines.

Physical aspects

- Sensitive reaction to pain • Headaches
- Facial pain and neuralgia • Palpitations
brought on by anger or stress • Skin that
reacts in a hypersensitive manner • Migraine.

Modalities

- **Better:** for warmth.
- **Worse:** for the open air and strong smells.

Treatment Tips

A good remedy for insomnia caused by too
much mental activity, particularly when
combined with an inability to relax.

D r o s e r a

Drosera is derived from a tiny plant that traps insects inside its leaves.

Treatment Use

Drosera is useful when any of the following are indicated:

Mental and emotional aspects

● Feelings of restlessness and anxiety when left alone ● Fear of ghosts ● Difficulty in concentrating ● Sense of persecution ● Prone to talkativeness ● Suspicious of bad or unwelcome news.

Physical aspects

● Colds, especially when accompanied by a violent cough ● Coughs that will not stop and are spasmodic ● Coughs accompanied by nausea or vomiting ● Whooping cough ● Joint pain and growing pains in the legs of teenagers if accompanied by symptoms of stiffness.

Modalities

● **Better:** for being outside in the fresh air and stretching the body and limbs.

● **Worse:** late at night, or lying down for long periods of time; after drinking and eating cold food, after periods of talking.

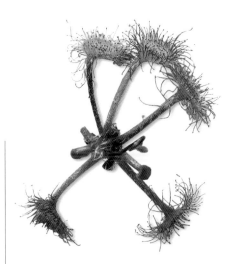

Drosera rotundifolia is a tiny plant found in bogs and heaths. The whole fresh plant in flower is used for the remedy.

Treatment Tips

An excellent remedy for coughs and colds, in particular for a dry, retching cough.

Drosera is good for joint pain and for "growing pains" of teenagers. The symptoms can be helped by stretching, especially outside.

Gelsemium

Gelsemium is derived from the yellow jasmine plant.

Treatment Use

Gelsemium is useful when any of the following are indicated:

Mental and emotional aspects

● Fears and phobias when accompanied by shaking and trembling ● Fear of dentists and doctors ● Fear of being left alone ● Anxiety about forthcoming events, such as meetings ● Drowsiness and confusion ● Panic attacks ● Dislike of insects and creatures that creep and crawl ● Difficulty in sleeping.

Physical aspects

● Influenza ● Sore throat with red tonsils ● Difficulty swallowing ● Fatigue, exhaustion, and drowsiness ● Coughs and colds ● Shivering ● Sneezing with a hot and flushed face ● Sore, inflamed eyes ● Migraine and headaches, in particular at the base of the skull or the back of the head ● Weakness and heaviness in the extremities ● Diarrhea that is made worse when anxious.

The climbing plant Carolina jasmine grows in parts of the United States. Its aromatic fresh roots are used in the remedy.

Modalities

● **Better:** for rest and stillness; after going to the toilet.
● **Worse:** for cold, damp weather.

Treatment Tips

The main remedy for influenza. Also excellent for coughs, colds, and sore throats, particularly if accompanied by shivering and fever.

This remedy is a useful addition to a homeopathic first-aid kit.

Gelsemium is used for fears and phobias that cause trembling. The remedy works on the spinal cord and respiratory system.

Graphites

Graphites is derived from the mineral graphite or black lead, which is commonly used for pencil leads.

Treatment Use

Graphites is useful when any of the following are indicated:

Mental and emotional aspects

● Fidgeting, in particular when nervous and anxious ● Easily triggered feelings of guilt ● Depression ● Indecisiveness ● Timidness ● Postmenopausal depression ● Bulimia.

Physical aspects

● Eczema, particularly behind the knees, on the wrist, inside and outside of ears ● Contact dermatitis, particularly on the palms of the hands and between the fingers ● Psoriasis ● Dry, cracked, and sore skin ● Itchiness or skin eruptions of the scalp ● Cold sores ● Stomach problems ● Cramp ● Constipation ● Styes ● Nail problems ● Chilblains ● Erratic menstrual cycle ● Morning headaches.

Modalities

● **Better:** for eating.
● **Worse:** for heat.

Graphites can be used to treat a wide range of complaints, including stomach problems and morning headaches.

Treatment Tips

Use to treat the first outbreak of skin complaints—in particular eczema and dermatitis, particularly where there is a discharge. In these cases, the remedy should be supported topically with an application of the homeopathic ointment or cream.

This remedy is a useful addition to a homeopathic first-aid kit.

Graphite is a carbon, the main constituent of pencils. The mineral graphite is ground into a powder to make the Graphites remedy.

Hamamelis

Hamamelis is derived from the witch-hazel plant. The twigs, bark, and outer layer of the root are used.

Treatment Use

Hamamelis is useful when any of the following are indicated:

Fresh bark, twigs, and the outer root of the witch-hazel plant (Hamamelis virginiana) are ground together and used for the remedy.

Mental and emotional aspects

- Mild depression; the person feels better for being alone • Irritability and restlessness, particularly in the presence of others.

Physical aspects

- Varicose veins • Varicocele (varicose veins in the testes) • Heavy and tired, throbbing and itching, or stinging and aching legs • Irritated and bloodshot eyes • Black eyes • Bruising • Chilblains • Nosebleeds • Mild skin rashes • Insect bites where accompanied with stinging and aching around the bite • Mild burns • Acne and oily skin • Hemorrhoids.

Modalities

- **Better:** for fresh air; for reading, thinking, or talking.
- **Worse:** for warm, damp heat and pressure; for movement.

Treatment Tips

Use at the first sign of varicose veins or hemorrhoids or when these conditions become worse. Treatment can be backed up with a cream or ointment applied directly onto the affected sites.

Hamamelis is excellent for both internal and external bleeding. It can be used to treat bruising of the body caused by injury.

Hepar sulf.

Hepar sulf. is derived from calcium sulfide.

Treatment Use

Hepar sulf. is useful when any of the following are indicated:

Mental and emotional aspects

● Irritation over the slightest matter ● Quick to take offense ● Talks quickly when anxious ● Overreacts when angry ● Prone to bouts of sadness and depression.

The remedy is prepared chemically by mixing calcium carbonate (derived from oyster shells) together with flowers of sulfur.

Physical aspects

● All skin problems that gather pus and are slow to heal ● Skin ulcers and bedsores ● Acne and boils ● Earache ● Ear pain with a sore throat ● Catarrh ● Coughs that create a hoarse and dry throat ● Cold sores, particularly around the eyes ● Mouth ulcers ● Influenza with sweating and sneezing ● Cracked, dry lips ● Perspiration that causes a bad odor, even when deodorant is used.

Treatment Tips

A good remedy to use when conditions are slow to heal. Good for clearing infection and discharges.

The Hepar sulf. remedy can be used to treat infections that cause earache. It helps to expel the discharge from the site of the infection.

Modalities

● **Better:** for warmth and for wrapping up and keeping the head warm.

● **Worse:** for touch and the cold.

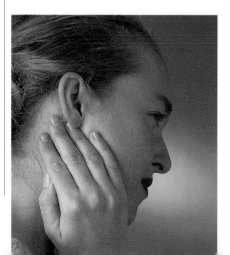

Hypericum

Hypericum is derived from the St. John's-wort herb.

Treatment Use

Hypericum is useful when any of the following are indicated:

Mental and emotional aspects

- Depression with tiredness and lethargy
- Depression after surgery or after injury • Vertigo • Shock through injury or emotional trauma
- Stress and anxiety that cause spasms and feelings of tightness in the body.

Physical aspects

- Neuralgia • Puncture wounds received from sharp objects (glass, nails, etc) • Splinters
- All wounds and injuries, in particular if crushing is involved • Concussion • Nerve pain or stabbing • Shooting pains • Injuries to the feet, hands, and spine • Minor eye injuries • Chronic back pain, with a sensation of pain traveling up and down the back
- Asthma when in a damp environment

The hypericum plant (Hypericum perforatum) produces a red juice from its flowers and leaves, which are used in the remedy.

- Toothache and pain from dental procedures
- Diarrhea • Hemorrhoids with pain and bleeding.

Modalities

- **Better:** for resting the head bent backward; for gentle massage.
- **Worse:** for cold, damp, and foggy weather.

Treatment Tips

A good remedy to use after an injury to the skin, particularly where there is a risk of infection.

This remedy is a useful addition to a homeopathic first-aid kit.

Hypericum can be used to treat nerve pain after injury.

Ignatia

Ignatia is derived from St Ignatius bean, a seedpod from the *Ignatia amara* tree.

Treatment Use

Ignatia is useful when any of the following are indicated:

Mental and emotional aspects

- Highly emotional states • Shock • Anger
- Grief • Inability to express emotions
- Hysteria • Insomnia • Quick, sudden tearfulness • Self-blame and self-pity
- Worry • Sadness over divorce and broken relationships • Sudden, unexpected mood changes • Exhaustion caused by overwork
- Obsessive-compulsive behavior
- Hypochondria • Jealousy • Fixed ideas.

Physical aspects

- Headaches caused by emotional stress and tension • Coughs and sore throats
- Difficulty in swallowing • Twitching of the face triggered by anxiety • Digestive problems, in particular after shock or grief when accompanied with a sinking sensation • Cravings for odd foods when ill
- Diarrhea • Disruptive sleep patterns, particularly if grieving.

The *Ignatia* remedy is made from the seeds of the Ignatia amara fruit. The seeds are ground to a powder.

Modalities

- **Better:** for warmth and the sun; change of position.
- **Worse:** in cold air; for emotional upset; in the morning.

Treatment Tips

One of the best remedies for emotional problems. It is good for mood swings, bereavement, and any accompanying physical ailments. It is also good if the ailments are very changeable.

Kali phos.

Kali phos. is derived from potassium phosphate.

Treatment Use

Kali phos. is useful when any of the following are indicated:

Mental and emotional aspects

- Complete exhaustion • Oversensitive reactions and nervousness when stressed
- Frustration due to lack of assertiveness
- Shyness and withdrawal when anxious
- Nervousness when meeting people
- Depression, including postviral depression • Nightmares • Lack of concentration and poor memory • Fear of a nervous breakdown.

The Kali phos. remedy is prepared chemically from potassium carbonate, derived from potash and dilute phosphoric acid.

Physical aspects

- Weakness of limbs • Neck and upper back pain • Tension headaches • Dizziness after rising from sitting or kneeling • Chronic fatigue syndrome • Discharges from colds and catarrh • Productive coughs • Diarrhea
- Cystitis.

Modalities

- **Better:** for heat and movement.
- **Worse:** for worry.

Treatment Tips

Known as the "great nerve soother," this is excellent in the treatment of all forms of exhaustion, particularly those brought on by stress.

Kali phos. can be used to treat neck and upper back pain and headaches caused by tension.

Lachesis

Lachesis is derived from the venom of
the bushmaster snake.

Treatment Use

Lachesis is useful when any of the following
are indicated:

*The fresh venom of the bushmaster snake can be dried
and made into the remedy.*

Mental and emotional aspects

- Hypersensitivity ● Talkative, rambling, self-
absorbed nature ● Restlessness ● Fixed ideas
and opinions, in particular about religion
- Fear of personal attack or burglary
- Suspicion of new people ● Jealousy and
suspicion of loved ones ● No desire to mix
with people ● Suppression of anger
- Nightmares ● Irritability ● Anger after
the break-up of relationships ● Addictions,
including alcohol, tobacco, and drugs
- Premenstrual syndrome ● Postmenopausal depression ● Panic attacks.

Physical aspects

- Headaches, particularly on waking
- Puffy, bloated, or swollen face ● Stomach-
ache when craving stimulants ● Constrictive,
sore throats ● Asthma ● Angina pain
- Palpitations and tightness or constriction
of the chest ● Hot flushes ● Bloatedness

● Varicose veins ● Hemorrhoids ● Varicocele
(varicose veins in the testes) ● Phlebitis and
thrombosis ● Menopausal problems.

Modalities

- **Better:** in the open air; for eating and
cool drinks.
- **Worse:** when trying to sleep;
for touch; for tight clothing

Treatment Tips

Excellent for all circulatory
problems. Also good for
extreme stress when
accompanied with pains and
tightness in the chest.

*Swollen, sore throats are helped
by Lachesis, which eases the pain and
makes it easier to take in fluids that
were previously difficult to swallow.*

Ledum

Ledum is derived from the
wild rosemary plant.

Treatment Use

Ledum is useful when any of the following
are indicated:

Mental and emotional aspects

- Sleep disturbance with night sweats
- Impatience • Timidness.

Physical aspects

- Feelings of hotness and swelling
triggered by stress • Wounds
- Stings with bruising and
puffiness • Grazes and cuts • Bites
- It can prevent cuts, bites, or stings from
becoming infected • Injury to the eyes
- Arthritic and rheumatic pain affecting the
ankles, knees, or lower legs • Hot, burning
sensations in the limbs • Gout.

Modalities

- **Better:** for cold compresses.
- **Worse:** at night; with heat.

*The Ledum remedy can be
used to help alleviate night
sweats and sleeplessness.*

Fresh, flowering wild rosemary plants (Ledum palustre) *are dried
and powdered to make the remedy.*

Treatment Tips

This is an ideal remedy for puncture wounds.
It can prevent any infection caused through
bites, stings, and cuts.

This remedy is a useful addition
to a homeopathic first-aid kit.

Lycopodium

Lycopodium is derived from the pollen dust of an evergreen herb.

The flowering spikes of the lycopodium herb provide yellow pollen dust, which is shaken out of the plant and used for the remedy.

Treatment Use

Lycopodium is useful when any of the following are indicated:

Mental and emotional aspects

- Lack of self-confidence ● Sexual fears
- Anxiety and fear of interviews and speeches
- Sensitivity ● Forgetfulness ● Irritation caused by minor matters ● Dislike of being contradicted ● Feelings of stress when meeting strangers ● Fear of ghosts, death, and the dark ● Dislike of being alone
- Suppression of fears ● Agoraphobia
- Chronic fatigue syndrome ● Nervous breakdown ● Bulimia.

Physical aspects

- Digestive disorders including indigestion, irritable bowel syndrome, nausea, ulcers, hunger pains, feeling bloated after little food, flatulence, constipation ● Impotence
- Sore throats ● Dry cough
- Extreme tiredness followed by colds or influenza ● Bladder and kidney problems, including kidney stones ● Prostate problems ● Hair loss ● Restless legs at night ● Cold hands and feet ● Headaches over the eyes ● Shoulder pain ● Varicose veins ● Chronic eczema.

Modalities

- **Better:** for small meals and movement.
- **Worse:** for heat and stuffy environment.

Treatment Tips

The first remedy to use for digestive disorders.

The Lycopodium remedy helps cure digestive complaints, particularly indigestion.

Merc. Sol.

Merc. sol. is derived from the black oxide of mercury.

Treatment Use

Merc. sol. is useful when any of the following are indicated:

Liquid mercury is dissolved in dilute nitric acid, forming a gray-black precipitate. This is used to make the remedy.

Mental and emotional aspects

- Slowness and sluggishness of thought
- Distrust of others • Fear of burglary and abuse • Poor memory and difficulty in recall
- Mental and emotional weakness and fatigue
- Chronic fatigue syndrome • Restlessness and anxiety • Deep insecurity
- Suspiciousness • Sensitivity to criticism
- Quick, sudden, and aggressive temper
- Lack of willpower • Tendency to be arrogant • Emotional repression.

Physical aspects

- Stammering • Dribbling from the mouth when sleeping • Tiredness in the limbs and feelings of weakness through the whole body • Body odor
- Cutting, burning pains • Gum and mouth problems • Mouth ulcers
- Bad taste in the mouth, in particular a metallic taste • Oral thrush • Sore throats
- Cold sores • Conjunctivitis with discharge
- Spasmodic coughs • Joint pain • Catarrh
- Scalp problems, eruptions, and crustiness of the scalp • Bed sores.

Modalities

- **Better:** for rest in moderate temperatures.
- **Worse:** at night; for heat or changes in temperature.

Treatment Tips

An excellent remedy for problems with the mouth, especially mouth ulcers and gum problems.

Merc. sol. can be used to treat mouth and throat complaints, including gingivitis, halitosis, and tonsillitis.

Natrum mur.

Natrum mur. is derived from a mineral rock salt called sodium chloride.

Treatment Use

Natrum mur. is useful when any of the following are indicated:

Mental and emotional aspects

- Anxiety and depression caused by suppressed grief ● Repressed fear
- Agoraphobia ● Fear of thunderstorms
- Hypochondria ● Agitation ● Guilt
- Anorexia ● Shock ● Low self-worth
- Premenstrual syndrome ● Quick changing of emotions without warning ● Resentment
- Tendency to sulk or keep feelings locked up.

Physical aspects

- Sunstroke ● Migraine ● Eye strain
- Cold sores ● Cracked and dry lips
- Mouth ulcers ● Inflamed gums ● Boils and warts ● Anemia ● Constipation ● Backache
- Irregular periods ● Hair loss ● Oily skin and hair ● Coughs and colds ● Palpitations.

Modalities

- **Better:** for cool, fresh air.
- **Worse:** for heat and sunlight; on waking.

Rock salt is the source of this remedy. It is formed by the evaporation of salty water, which leaves a thick, salty crust behind.

Treatment Tips

A good remedy for people who brood on the past. Very good for treating emotional trauma, such as anxiety or depression caused by loss, grief, or separation.

The Natrum mur. remedy may help a fear of thunderstorms. Symptoms of anxiety may be made worse by thundery weather.

Nux vomica

Nux vomica is derived from the poison strychnine, which is extracted from the seeds of the *Strychnos nux vomica* tree.

The leaves, bark, and seeds of the Strychnos nux vomica tree all contain strychnine, but it is usually extracted from the dried seeds.

Treatment Use

Nux vomica is useful when any of the following are indicated:

Mental and emotional aspects

● Tendency to overindulge ● Cravings for stimulants such as alcohol, tobacco, and rich foods ● Addictive nature ● Fear of failure ● Argumentative ● Critical ● Fear of spiders and beetles ● Dread of death ● Depression ● Insomnia ● Hyperactivity ● Frustration.

Physical aspects

● Digestive problems, such as indigestion and heartburn ● Food poisoning ● Vomiting ● Constipation ● Diarrhea ● Stomach cramps ● Lower back pain ● Hiccups ● Headaches and migraines ● Hay fever ● Colds and influenza ● Blocked nose ● Heavy, aching muscles ● Fragility ● Morning sickness and cramp in pregnancy.

Modalities

● **Better:** for sleep.
● **Worse:** in the morning.

Treatment Tips

Excellent "hangover" remedy. Also good for aiding digestion and promoting the appetite.

This remedy is a useful addition to a homeopathic first-aid kit.

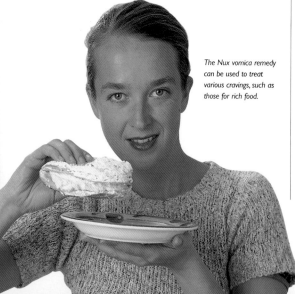

The Nux vomica remedy can be used to treat various cravings, such as those for rich food.

Phosphorus

Phosphorus is derived from a mineral found in phosphates and living matter. It's found in bones, teeth, and bodily fluids.

Treatment Use

Phosphorus is useful when any of the following are indicated:

Mental and emotional aspects

- Hypersensitivity • Excessive imagination
- Easily angered • Fear of darkness and death
- Suppression of fear • Fixed ideas • Fatigue
- Craving for reassurance • Unnecessary worry about health • Nightmares and insomnia • Facial twitches • Shock
- Low spirits • Clairvoyant episodes
- Preference for company and fear of loneliness.

Physical aspects

- Unproductive, hard, dry cough with a tight, heavy chest • Low resistance to infections
- Sore throat with hoarseness • Pneumonia
- Bronchitis • Feels the cold • Asthma
- Bruising • Nose bleeds • Bleeding gums
- Heavy periods • Headaches • Vertigo
- Styes • Panic attacks • Exhaustion and fatigue • Food poisoning • Heartburn

Phosphorus is a yellowish non-metallic mineral, derived from phosphates and living matter.

- Back pain with a burning, hot sensation
- Dandruff • Weakness in the extremities.

Modalities

- **Better:** for warm, fresh air; touch and rubbing.
- **Worse:** for overexertion; at night.

Treatment Tips

This is the ideal remedy for relieving ailments that are triggered by fear and anxiety as it helps to soothe the nervous system.

The symptoms helped by the Phosphorus remedy may be further alleviated by massage or rubbing.

Pulsatilla

Pulsatilla is derived from the pulsatilla plant, which is native to Scandinavia, Denmark, Germany, and Russia. The fresh plant in flower is used.

Treatment Use

Pulsatilla is useful when any of the following are indicated:

Mental and emotional aspects

● Tendency to burst into tears without warning ● Quiet temperament ● Suppression of fear ● Depression ● Obsessive-compulsive behavior ● Fear of the opposite sex ● Fear of the dark and ghosts ● Very tearful when grieving ● Bulimia.

Physical aspects

● Coughs and colds ● Runny nose ● Catarrh ● Conjunctivitis ● Digestive problems ● Irritable bowel syndrome ● All menstrual and menopausal problems, particularly if accompanied

The flowers of the pulsatilla plant Pulsatilla nigricans are crushed for their juices, which are used to make the remedy.

by depression ● Lower back pain ● Headaches ● Varicose veins ● Arthritis ● Styes ● Incontinence ● Skin problems.

Modalities

● **Better:** for crying and sympathy; cool, fresh air; gentle exercise.

● **Worse:** for heat; for rich or fatty foods.

Treatment Tips

This remedy works well on the mental state of the individual.

The Pulsatilla remedy is useful for depression and weepiness.

R h u s   t o x .

Rhus tox. is derived from the fresh
leaves of the poison ivy plant.

The leaves are collected from the poison ivy plant before
it flowers and are pulped to make the remedy.

Treatment Use

Rhus tox. is useful when any of the following
are indicated:

Mental and emotional aspects

- Irritability ● Depression ● Suicidal thoughts
- Lack of joy in life ● Anxiousness ● Fear of
being poisoned ● Anxiety at night.

Physical aspects

- Skin problems, including eczema, dermatitis,
and blistering ● Burning, itching, swollen skin
- Cold sores ● Diaper rash ● Sciatica
- Chicken pox ● Shingles ● Influenza
- Sore, stinging eyes ● Muscular aches and

pains ● Stiffness ● Joint pain ● Back pain
● Arthritis and rheumatism ● Sprains and
strains ● Jaw pain ● Frozen shoulder
● Neuralgia ● Postoperative recovery
● Repetitive strain injury.

Modalities

- **Better:** for movement; for a warm,
dry atmosphere.
- **Worse:** for rest and stillness; for cold,
damp weather.

Treatment Tips

This is an excellent remedy for muscular aches
and pains. Eczema and other skin problems
often respond to this remedy when others fail.

This remedy is a useful addition
to a homeopathic first-aid kit.

The Rhus tox. remedy may help repetitive strain injury, which can
be caused by spending long hours using a computer keyboard.

Ruta grav.

Ruta grav. is derived from the *Ruta graveolens* herb. The juice from the whole plant is used, before the plant flowers.

Treatment Use

Ruta grav. is useful when any of the following are indicated:

Mental and emotional aspects

- Low personal satisfaction
- Depression ● Critical of others and self ● Anxiety.

Physical aspects

- Aches and pains in bones and muscles ● Deep, aching pain
- Arthritis and rheumatism ● Lower back pain, where the pain feels deep and penetrating ● Repetitive strain injury
- Injuries to ligaments, tendons, and cartilage
- Sciatic pain ● Chest and rib pain caused by coughing ● Eye strain and exhaustion from overwork ● Headaches, in particular from reading ● Constipation.

Modalities

- **Better:** for movement.
- **Worse:** for cold, damp weather; lying down.

Juice is extracted from the whole plant (Ruta graveolens) before it flowers.

Treatment Tips

This remedy acts upon the periosteum (the lining of the bone) and cartilage, so it is excellent for injuries to gliding joints such as the ankle and wrist. This remedy is also the first choice for repetitive strain injury—an inflammation of the tendon sheaths of the arm and wrist.

Ruta grav. can be used for deep aching pain and rheumatism. Damp weather can make the symptoms of such conditions worse.

Sepia

Sepia is derived from the ink of
the cuttlefish.

Treatment Use

Sepia is useful when any of the following
are indicated:

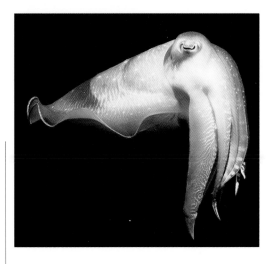

The cuttlefish squirts a dark ink for its protection. The pigments
from the ink are used to make the remedy.

Mental and emotional aspects

- Menopausal depression
- Exhaustion and slowness of
thought • Feelings of
weakness • Tendency to
cry easily • Stress and
anxiety • Feelings of
being unable to cope
• Fear of sickness and
disease • Fixed ideas
• Irritability • Grief,
particularly on separation or
relationship break-ups.

Physical aspects

- Chronic fatigue syndrome
- Menopausal problems,
including hot flushes and night
sweats • Ovarian, vaginal, and

The Sepia remedy can be used to treat hot
flushes during the menopause.

uterine complaints, including prolapse of the
uterus • Heavy periods • Thrush • Backache
• Flatulence and abdominal and stomach
tenderness • Headaches and migraines
• Constipation • Hemorrhoids and varicose
veins • Hair loss • Tiredness • Dizziness
• Sweaty feet.

Modalities

- **Better:** for sleep; warmth; gentle exercise.
- **Worse:** in the morning; for a sedentary
lifestyle.

Treatment Tips

An excellent remedy for women, because it
helps greatly with menopausal problems. It is
also good for exhaustion.

Silicea

Silicea is derived from the main part of most rocks and plant stems. It is also found in teeth, hair, and bones. This remedy is mainly derived from quartz or flint.

Treatment Use

Silicea is useful when any of the following are indicated:

Rock crystal is a type of quartz. Traditionally, quartz or flint have been used to prepare the remedy.

Mental and emotional aspects

* Low self-confidence ● Fear of failure ● Lack of assertiveness and timidity ● Anxiety about important events
* Exhaustion after periods of concentration
* Performance fear
* Obsessiveness about detail ● Stubbornness
* Fear of commitment.

Physical aspects

* Weak immune system
* Weak nervous system
* Slowness of healing, particularly broken bones and fractures ● Recurrent

The Silicea remedy can be used for helping fractured bones to heal.

coughs, colds, and respiratory infections
● Ear infections ● Sore, throbbing throat
● Swelling of glands ● Catarrh ● Chest infections, especially if a family history of tuberculosis ● Boils ● Headaches, especially if triggered by cold ● Painful joints and bones
● Anorexia and undernourishment in general
● Unhealthy skin, including acne ● Slow bone growth in babies and children ● Light-sensitive eyes ● Poor sense of smell ● Cracking at the corner of the mouth ● Sensitive gums
● Constipation ● Sweaty feet and head.

Modalities

* **Better:** for keeping warm.
* **Worse:** for cold, damp weather; drafts.

Treatment Tips

A good remedy to use if an individual has low resistance to disease and is slow to recover from infection.

Staphysagria

Staphysagria is derived from the seed of the plant sometimes known as stavesacre or palmated larkspur. It was used by the Greeks and Romans as a remedy.

Treatment Use

Staphysagria is useful when any of the following are indicated:

Mental and emotional aspects

- Suppression of emotions, in particular anger
- Outbursts of temper • Fixated about an illness, symptom, or emotional problem
- Likes to be alone • Sensitive to criticism and easily offended • Resentment and jealousy • Hypersensitivity • Sex addiction
- Workaholic • Overindulgence in alcohol, tobacco, or food.

The seeds of the Delphinium staphysagria plant are used to make the remedy.

Physical aspects

- Postoperative trauma • Enlargement of prostate gland • Skin problems • Headaches
- Flatulence • Teething problems • Neuralgia
- Styes • Inflammation of the eyes

Modalities

- **Better:** for warmth.
- **Worse:** for suppressing emotions; touch.

Treatment Tips

It can be used to treat suppressed emotions and anger, and diseases stemming from these.

The remedy Staphysagria can be used to control suppressed rage.

Sulfur

Sulfur is derived from the mineral sulfur.

Treatment Use

Sulfur is useful when any of the following are indicated:

Mental and emotional aspects

• Forgetfulness • Inability to think clearly • Lack of regard for others • Laziness • Irritability • Self-centeredness and selfishness • Argumentative • Aggressive tendencies • Claustrophobia • Fear of heights (vertigo) • Fear of oppression • Bulimia • Insomnia • Postmenopausal depression • Alcoholism • Addiction to smoking • Lack of willpower • Nightmares.

Physical aspects

• Burning, itching skin • Eczema, dermatitis, psoriasis • Thrush • Diaper rash • Catarrh • Hot, sweaty burning feet • Digestive disorders • Constipation • Diarrhea • Indigestion • Loss of appetite • Hemorrhoids • Lower back pain • Gout • Headaches • Conjunctivitis • Red, sore, and itchy eyes • Offensive body

A powder called flowers of sulfur is extracted from the mineral sulfur and used to make the remedy.

odor • Menopausal problems such as hot flushes and dizziness • Hair loss • Dry, itchy scalp • Dry lips • Sore throats • Stiff knees and ankles.

Modalities

• **Better:** for warm, fresh air.
• **Worse:** early mornings and late nights; damp, cold weather; washing; prolonged sitting and standing.

Treatment Tips

Skin problems, particularly where the skin is red and itchy (such as eczema), respond well to this remedy. It is also a good general remedy for detoxification.

The remedy Sulfur can be used to treat skin conditions such as diaper rash.

Thuja

Thuja is derived from the leaves and twigs of the evergreen conifer tree, which is commonly known as the white cedar tree.

Treatment Use

Thuja is useful when any of the following are indicated:

Mental and emotional aspects

● Anorexia ● Distorted ideas of body image ● Fear of strangers ● Facial twitches ● Fixed ideas ● Anxiety ● Cries easily ● Dyslexia ● Paranoia ● Interrupted sleep ● Lack of self-esteem ● Secretive ● Manipulative but weak.

Physical aspects

● Warts ● Verrucas ● Skin complaints ● Very oily skin ● Acne ● Perspiration with odor ● Headaches ● Polyps of the nose ● Styes ● Nail problems ● Hemorrhoids ● Loss of appetite ● Constantly cold ● Urethral and vaginal infections ● Menstrual problems including cramps.

Modalities

● **Better:** for movement.
● **Worse:** for cold and damp; at night.

The leaves and twigs of the arborvitae conifer (Thuja occidentalis) are pounded to make the remedy.

Treatment Tips

Thuja is the first remedy of choice for dealing with warts and verrucas. In addition, it can be applied topically to provide backup to the oral treatment.

In addition to its use in dealing with warts, verrucas, and other skin complaints, Thuja remedy can be used to combat loss of appetite.

Zinc. Met.

Zinc. met. is derived from zinc.

Treatment Use

Zinc. met. is useful when any of the following are indicated:

Mental and emotional aspects

- Mental fatigue ● Poor memory
- Restlessness ● Depression ● Alcoholism
- Irritability ● Jumpiness ● Constant fidgeting.

Physical aspects

- Exhaustion ● Restless legs ● Tiredness through lack of sleep ● Weakness and exhaustion ● Head feels heavy ● Chilblains ● Cramp ● Varicose veins ● Chronic fatigue syndrome ● Bulimia ● Sensitivity to noise ● Anemia.

Modalities

- **Better:** for bowel movement; emotional reassurance.
- **Worse:** after food.

Treatment Tips

A good remedy for lack of vitality or for treating exhaustion. It is also good for constant feelings of coldness.

Zinc is a bluish metal; it is ground up to make the powder from which the remedy is made.

Zinc. met. may help to restore vitality.

Topical Applications

Some homeopathic remedies can be used in preparations that are applied directly to the skin. These are known as topical applications and are an ideal way to back up the oral remedies. They can also be used on their own or as a first-aid treatment. Topical treatments come in the forms listed below.

Forms of Topical Treatments

Creams: Easily absorbed.

Ointments: Greasier than creams in texture; best for larger areas.

Tinctures: Liquid remedies ready for dilution in water; best for cuts and grazes. Dilute according to instructions.

Massage balms: Remedies in vegetable oil base, ready for massage.

Sprays: Ready-mixed; useful for insect bites and stings (e.g., pyrethrum spray).

The following remedies are the most widely available topical applications and are listed with the conditions they are usually used to treat.

Arnica: Bruising. Muscular aches and pains. Sprains and strains. After sport or exercise. Joint pain. Aching and stiff back. Tired, aching feet. First signs of repetitive strain injury. Frozen shoulder. Neck pain and stiffness. Sunburn (but do not apply to broken skin).

Calendula: Sensitive, dry, irritated, cracked, and inflamed skin. Acne. Contact dermatitis. Eczema. Rashes. Cradle cap. Cold sores. Razor burn. Sunburn. Can be used on babies for minor irritations such as diaper rash and grazes. Good for cleaning cuts and wounds. Can be used as a facial moisturizer or aftershave balm.

Graphites: Eczema. Contact dermatitis. Psoriasis. Varicose eczema, or to help prevent it where skin is dry, thin, and translucent. Extremely dry, itchy, sore skin. Sore skin in and around the nose accompanied by a cold. Cold sores. Use as a facial moisturizer to help clear eczema, dermatitis, or allergic reaction to cosmetics.

Hamamelis: Sore, burning, itching skin. Varicose veins. Phlebitis. Hemorrhoids. Heavy, aching legs and feet, in particular after long periods of standing. *Always apply lightly around varicose sites. Do not use on broken skin.*

Hypericum: Cuts, sores, wounds, scrapes, and grazes. Cold sores. Itchy, irritated, and inflamed skin. Splinters. Nail irritations (nail-bed cuts or bitten, sore nails). Cracked, sore lips. Blisters. Sore, bleeding hemorrhoids.

Rhus tox.: Muscular aches and pains, in particular from physical overexertion. Repetitive strain injury. Joint pain, including tennis elbow and knee injuries. Arthritis and rheumatism. Sciatica. Useful to use after Arnica, once the bruising has diminished. *Do not apply to broken skin.*

Ruta grav.: Stiffness and pain in tendons, ligaments, joints, and muscles where there is a deep aching. Repetitive strain injury. Sciatica. Rib and chest pain brought on by coughs. Good for sports-related ankle and wrist pain. *Do not apply to broken skin.*

Thuja: Warts. Verrucas. Brittle, weak nails.

First-aid and Travel Kit

 A homeopathic first-aid kit is a very useful item to have around the house, in the car, or on vacation. Make sure it is readily available. You may wish to purchase a remedy box in which to store your first-aid kit.

Several homeopathic pharmacies and suppliers provide a ready-made first-aid kit. Some of these consist of up to 18 remedies in small bottles or vials. It may not be necessary for you to have this many remedies. Look at the remedies listed in this section and decide which ones would be most useful. You may have already used some of the remedies or have worked out your constitutional type, and therefore know which ones work well for you.

KIT REMEDIES

The following ten remedies would normally be enough to treat most first-aid situations.

Aconite

Panic. Fear. Pain. First signs of a cold or sore throat and fever.

Inability to relax. Anxiety. To help induce sleep after a long journey. Any condition with a sudden onset.

Apis mel.

For bites and stings. Fluid retention and swelling. Swelling of legs and feet when traveling.

Arnica

Shock. Injury. Bruising. Neck, back, shoulder, and joint pain. Sprains and strains. Headaches. Jet lag. Topical application of Arnica cream or ointment can be used for bruising, sprains, strains, and sunburn (but not on broken skin).

Cantharis

Chronic cystitis. Burning, stinging pain. Insect bites and stings. Sunburn..

Gelsemium

Sore throats. Coughs and colds. Influenza with shivering.

Graphites

Allergies. Reactions or break-outs of the skin due to change of climate or change of washing powders. Reactions to swimming-pool chemicals. Eczema. Dermatitis. Topical application of Graphites cream can be used to soothe eczema, dermatitis or itchy, irritated skin.

Hypericum/Calendula mixture

Tincture for cleaning cuts and wounds. Ointment or cream for application on wounds, cuts, and grazes, or insect bites and stings.

Ledum

Puncture wounds. Splinters. Bites and stings.

Nux vomica

Food poisoning. Travel sickness. Upset stomach. Jet lag. Hangover. Over-indulgence in rich foods.

Rhus tox.

Muscular aches and pains. Stiffness and over-exertion. Back and joint pain. Muscular aches and pain. Useful after skiing, trekking, or activity vacations. The topical application of Rhus tox. can be used for muscular aches and pains, after sport or other exertion.

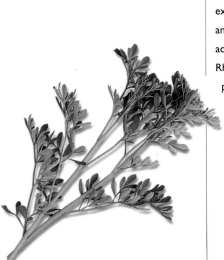

Useful Addresses and Websites

Please note that some homeopaths prefer not to have their address or telephone number listed on registers. Always check the qualifications of your homeopath. Personal recommendation is always the best way to find a good homeopath, but the following organizations may also help:

Homeopathic Organizations
American Association of Homeopathic
Pharmacists
P.O. Box 2273
Falls Church, VA 22042

American Board of Homeotherapeutics
1500 Massachusetts Ave., NW
Washington, D.C. 20005

American Institute of Homeopathy
1500 Massachusetts Ave., NW
Washington, D.C. 20005

Foundation for Homeopathic Education
and Research
2124 Kittredge St.
Berkeley, CA 94704
(510) 649-8930

International Foundation for Homeopathy
2366 Eastlake Ave.,
No.301 Seattle, WA 98102
(206) 324-8230

National Center for Homeopathy
801 North Fairfax St.
Suite 306
Alexandria, VA 22314
(703) 548-7790

If you have trouble obtaining your remedy from a local pharmacist, or health store, then try the suppliers below. Most will supply ointments, creams, and tinctures as well as the homeopathic tablets, boxes, and carry cases.

Suppliers of Homeopathic Medicines
Biological Homeopathic Industries (BHI)
11600 Cochiti S.E.
Albuquerque, NM 87123
(800) 621-7644

Boericke and Tafel, Inc.
2381 Circadian Way
Santa Rosa, CA 95407
(707) 571-8202

Boiron-Borneman
1208 Amosland Road
Norwood, PA 19074
(215) 532-2035

Dolisos America, Inc.
3014 Rigel Ave.
Las Vegas, NV 89102
(702) 871-7153

Hahnemann Pharmacy
828 San Pablo
Albany, CA 94706
(510) 527-3003

Homeopathic Educational Services
2124 Kittredge St.
Berkeley, CA 94704
(510) 649-0294

Humphreys Pharmacal Co.
63 Meadow Road
Rutherford, NJ 07070
(201) 933-7744

Luyties Pharmacal Co.
4200 Laclede Ave.
St. Louis, MO 63108
(800) 325-8080

Standard Homeopathic Company
P.O. Box 61607
436 W. Eighth Street
Los Angeles, CA 90014
(213) 321-4284

Washington Homeopathic Pharmacy
4914 Del Ray Ave.
Bethesda, MD 20814
(301) 656-1695

Weinstock Brauer Pharmaceuticals, Inc.
100 East Thousand Oaks Blvd.,
Suite 265, Thousand Oaks,
CA 91360
(805) 495-6704

Weleda, Inc.
841 South Main Street
Spring Valley, NY 10977

essential oils

Introduction

Humans love aromatic plants. When we pass a beautiful, scented flower our behavior shows this very clearly. The fragrance is enough to stop us in our tracks, making us forget our train of thought and plunge our face into the petals to inhale the perfume. When we do, we forget the cares and troubles of the day for a moment, and the world seems to be a simpler place. Gardeners love to touch and smell the herbs and aromatic grasses that they grow themselves, sniffing the aromas that cling to the fingers, such as pungent rosemary or zesty peppermint, fresh lavender or tangy fennel. These mouthwatering scents make us relax and breathe deeply.

All these perfumes we are inhaling and enjoying so enthusiastically are essential oils, the natural fragrances of aromatic plants. These scents are manufactured by the plants

The pungent herb rosemary uplifts the senses and excites the tastebuds. It is easily grown in a pot outside.

themselves and held in their tissues, only to be released through touch or the heat of the sun. Of all the plants on the Earth, only about one percent contain essential oils. Humans have enjoyed a special relationship with these species since antiquity, and we have used such plants for perfumes, incense, and medicines.

Flowers attract our sense of smell like a magnet. We are drawn to plants such as scented roses.

Aromatherapy relies on essential oils to achieve gentle, nurturing effects on body and mind. The oils are used on the skin, in the bath, and through inhalation to promote

Relaxing in a bath with essential oils soothes the senses and can bring relief from aches and pains in the body.

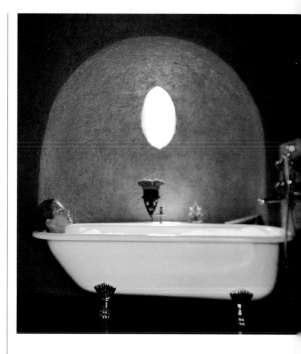

relaxation and well-being. Essential oils and aromatherapy can make a very positive contribution to emotional and physical health, bringing a sense of inner peace and balance.

This section of the book takes you on a journey through the world of essential oils, explaining where they come from and how they are obtained. It is an exploration of the particular plants that produce essential oils, revealing their unique role as a natural healing resource. The Essential Oils Index on pages 81–117 lists 36 common essential oils in detail, helping you get to know more about them and how to use them on yourself, friends, and family. The methods are straightforward and easy to use in everyday situations. You will also find information about safety issues, buying and keeping the oils, and simple skincare routines.

You may well find that collecting essential oils, enjoying their aromas, and learning about their different uses, becomes a fascinating pastime, that develops from being a hobby into, quite simply, a way of life.

This section links the essential oils to the plants from which they are extracted. The botanical emphasis of this approach helps us to remember that all life on Earth is dependent on plants. As custodians of the planet, we need to use these natural resources in a sustainable way if we are to continue to enjoy them.

Peppercorns yield a warming and stimulating essential oil that can ease painful joints and muscles.

How and Where are Essential Oils Obtained?

The production of essential oils involves a considerable investment of time, labor, and skill. Plants are cultivated, harvested, and processed to produce oils, which may then be shipped vast distances before reaching the consumer. Essential oils are a natural resource dependent on correct balances of soil composition, sun, and rain to achieve good harvests year by year—just like any other natural crop.

Many essential oils are found in distant locations world-wide. Mediterranean plants need sunlight to develop properly.

Geography

Essential oils are found in different plant groups all over the world. One of the most common is the botanical family *Labiatae*, which includes many Mediterranean plants such as rosemary, marjoram, and lavender. Most of the oils used in aromatherapy come from plants grown in southern Europe and North Africa, as these need a lot of sunlight to produce their oils. The same geographical region is the home of many citrus fruits in the *Rutaceae* family, including succulent oranges, lemons, and mandarins, whose peel is full of essential oil.

Farther afield you find the trees, flowers, and spices of India, for example, producer of jasmine, sandalwood, cardamom, and patchouli oils. Indonesia produces some of the more unusual oils, such as vetiver, which has a smoky, earthy aroma. The best geranium oil comes from the island of Réunion in the Indian Ocean, while Australia is the biggest producer of tea tree oil.

Cardamom pods produce a warm, fragrant, and spicy essential oil.

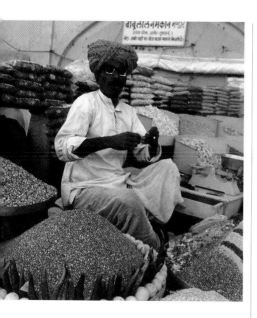

When buying an oil, check the Essential Oil Index (see pages 81–117) to see where it is produced and just how far it has traveled!

Cultivation

The cultivation of essential oils requires a lot of land to produce bulk supplies of plants. For example, it takes approximately half a metric ton of lavender material to produce just 4 cups (1 liter) of essential oil. Successful lavender farms need many acres of land.

Oils like vetiver are produced in developing countries where farmers use high levels of manual labor and traditional techniques. Very often the labor lies in the collection process where plants cannot be harvested

India is a huge producer of spices, aromatics, and fragrances. Some of the more unusual oils come from this great continent.

mechanically. In Bulgaria, roses are picked off the bush by hand—roughly 50–100 rose blooms are used for one drop of essential oil.

More mechanized essential oil cultivation is found in Australia, where tea tree oil is produced on a large scale on plantations using modern machinery for harvesting.

Extraction Methods

Essential oils are held in sacs or special microscopic cells within the plant tissues themselves. To extract the oil, different techniques are used:

Steam distillation passes steam at high pressure through the plant material, releasing the globules of essential oil into the water vapor. The fragrant steam is cooled back to water, and the essential oil can then be skimmed off as it floats on the surface. This technique is used to extract most oils, including lavender and rosemary.

Expression involves pressing the oil directly out of citrus fruit peel.

Solvent extraction uses chemical solvents to dissolve aromatic compounds out of delicate plant tissues. The extract is refined to produce an "absolute." Jasmine oil is produced by solvent extraction.

What are Essential Oils Used For?

In the last ten years, more and more people have been using essential oils and aromatherapy has become very popular. However, it may surprise you to discover that essential oils have a long history of use, both in aromatherapy and in other areas.

Ancient Egyptian men and women used aromatic fragrances to perfume the body and the hair.

Perfumery

Essential oils have been the basic ingredients in perfume formulae since the invention of a form of distillation by Avicenna, an Arab perfumer, mystic, and herbalist, at the beginning of the last millennium. Even before that, essential oils were extracted by a method called enfleurage, in which aromatic plant material was pressed into trays of fat, which were then heated in an oven or left out in the sun. The melted fat was strained and then left to set, and the solid, scented "unguent" used as a fragrance on the skin and hair.

In the past, only the most wealthy could afford the rare and costly extracts that were available. Perfumes were a sign of wealth and status. At the beginning of the twentieth century, the development of synthetic aromatic chemicals meant that perfume formulae could be copied, which is what happens in the mass production of fragrances today. Natural essential oils and aromatic extracts continue to be used for the creation of new formulae for perfumes, which are then synthetically reproduced.

Peppermint oil is used to flavor confectionery, including chocolates.

Food Flavoring

Many of the foodstuffs and drinks that we consume are flavored with essential oils. Obvious examples include the use of peppermint and citrus oils in chocolate and other confectionery. However, many oils are used to give "natural" flavors and fragrances to food products. They are used in preserved meats, alcoholic drinks, pickles, and sauces. The amounts of essential oil used are very small and are carefully monitored to be at safe levels for internal consumption, because essential oils are extremely concentrated. In aromatherapy, essential oils are never swallowed. (See "Essential Oil Safety Guidelines," pages 78–79.)

Pharmaceuticals

As well as being used in many foodstuffs, peppermint oil is used in pharmaceutical products such as toothpaste. Other essential oils that have pharmaceutical purposes include camphor and eucalyptus, which are used in commercial cough medicines, chest rubs, and ointments for muscular aches and pains. Many of these products have been licensed since the early twentieth century.

Aromatherapy

Of all the tons of essential oils produced world-wide each year, only about five to ten percent are used in aromatherapy. This is often a surprise to people, because they may be aware of essential oils only as the main ingredient in aromatherapy and not realize that they are so widely used elsewhere. In aromatherapy, it is very important that the oils used are totally natural and unadulterated with synthetics —trustworthy suppliers will buy directly from growers all around the world (for suppliers, see page 125).

Essential oils such as that found in the citrus fruit orange are often used as food flavorings and preservatives.

Essential oils such as peppermint or fennel are used to flavor different kinds of toothpaste the world over.

Essential Oil Safety Guidelines

Essential oils are completely natural. However, it is important to be aware that they are highly concentrated and need to be used safely and correctly. These guidelines will help you to check how to use essential oils in particular situations. It is advisable to consult your medical practitioner if you have any physical or psychological symptoms, as essential oils are not a replacement for professional medical treatment.

No to Oral Use

The most important safety guideline is simply this: do not take essential oils by mouth. They are highly concentrated substances and in large amounts they can do internal damage. If oils have been swallowed accidentally, seek medical help immediately.

Pregnancy Care

If you are pregnant, lactating, or breastfeeding, it is especially important not to swallow any essential oils. Any oils you use on yourself for massage or in the bath should be in very weak dilutions. If you are making any of the blends in this book, you should use half the

Women who are pregnant or breastfeeding need to be very careful when using essential oils.

stated number of drops. You are best advised to use flower and fruit oils only, as these are very gentle. It is a good idea to consult a qualified aromatherapist for advice.

Skin Safety

Before being applied to the skin, essential oils should always be diluted in a carrier oil such as sweet almond or grapeseed because they are so concentrated. Provided that you do not have sensitive skin (a tendency to allergic reactions), you can use lavender or tea tree neat for first-aid purposes (two drops on a cotton swab applied to the affected area). If you are sensitive to nuts, it is best to avoid sweet almond oil and use grapeseed instead.

Phototoxic Oils

Essential oils from the citrus fruits—bergamot, grapefruit, orange, lemon, lime, and mandarin— contain an ingredient that can cause skin

Only tea tree and lavender essential oils should be used neat on the skin. Other oils are not safe for such use.

reactions in sunlight. If you massage a blend with citrus oils into your skin, avoid direct exposure to strong UV light or a sunbed for 12 hours after application. This caution does not apply to inhalations or vaporizations with these oils.

High Blood Pressure

Rosemary essential oil is very stimulating and should be avoided if you have high blood pressure. Calming oils like lavender or ylang ylang are preferred for their soothing effects.

Epilepsy and Asthma

Again, rosemary essential oil has the potential to slightly increase the frequency of epileptic seizures, so it should be avoided by people with epilepsy. Calming oils like sandalwood, neroli, or orange are more appropriate. (Never attempt to apply oils during a seizure.) If you have asthma, it is advisable not to do inhalations with essential oils—use them for bathing, vaporization, and massage.

Babies and Children

Correct dosage of essential oils is especially crucial because of the delicate skin of small children. Follow these recommendations:

Babies up to 2 years: one drop of roman chamomile **or** rose otto **or** lavender in 4 teaspoons (20 ml) sweet almond carrier oil for general skin care and baby massage.

Children 2–10 years: any blends made from this book should contain half the stated number of drops. If an odd number of drops is given, reduce this to just under half (e.g. reduce 3 drops to 1, or 5 to 2).

Children over the age of 10: can receive oils in the same dilutions as adults.

Elderly Skin

In cases where the skin is delicate and very transparent with visible veins, you should use half the stated number of drops in any blend you make from this book so that the skin is nourished by the oils more gently.

Blends for children (and the elderly) contain low amounts of essential oils. Young skin is sensitive while older skin is more delicate.

How Essential Oils are Used in Aromatherapy

Aromatherapy is what it says it is—the "aroma" being the fragrances of essential oils, and the "therapy" the way in which the fragrance is applied to relieve physical symptoms and promote mental well-being. There are several simple ways to use essential oils, including in baths, inhalation, and massage.

Baths

For a 20-minute soak to relieve tension and stress, run the bath to a comfortable temperature. Sprinkle 4 drops maximum of one essential oil or 3 drops each of two essential oils as a combination onto the surface of the water. Agitate the water gently to disperse the oils before getting in. If you have dry or sensitive skin, you can dilute the essential oils in 4 teaspoons (20 ml) whole milk or unfragranced bath oil before adding to the water. A relaxing combination is 3 drops each of lavender and sandalwood.

Inhalation

This method helps to relieve colds, influenza, or sinus problems. You need a large bowl just over half full of nearly boiling water. Sprinkle 2 drops each of eucalyptus and tea tree onto the surface, then cover your head with a towel and inhale the aromatic steam for 15–20 minutes. Remove your glasses or contact lenses so they don't steam up or irritate the eyes.

Using steam inhalation can help to ease colds or blocked sinuses. Always be very careful when using boiling water.

Vaporization

Vaporizers gently heat up to evaporate the essential oil and disperse its fragrance into a room. You can buy a ceramic burner with tea light candles or one of the many electric models available. You should follow the manufacturer's guidelines when using the oils though; generally 4 drops of one oil or 3 drops each of two as a combination will scent a room for up to two hours. You can use tea tree and lemon essential oils to remove unpleasant odors, or choose a favorite aroma to create an environment that suits your mood.

An electrically powered fragrance diffuser can help ease breathing problems and is safe to be left on.

Choose the essential oil that meets your particular need, then blend with massage oil, bathe with it, or use in an inhalation.

Massage

When using essential oils for massage, they first need to be diluted in a carrier oil. These are vegetable oils such as grapeseed, sweet almond, or jojoba. Most of the massage blends in this book are based on a formula of using 10 drops of essential oils in 4 teaspoons (20 ml) carrier oil. The mixture should be stored in a clean glass bottle. Shake the mixture before use. This is a suitable dilution for massage on most skins and is enough to massage a full body, not including the face. Sensitive, very young, or elderly skin requires only 5 drops in 4 teaspoons (20 ml). (See pages 120–121 for Special Massage Blends.) Your blends will last for a maximum of four weeks. If you want to make larger quantities, simply take 8 teaspoons (40 ml) base oil and double the drops of essential oils in the blend formula.

Essential Oil Index

In this section, you will find 36 essential oils grouped according to the plant parts that produce them. Each essential oil file contains key information and blends to try out yourself to help ease physical conditions and rebalance mental and emotional states.

Root Oils

The energy of these oils is generally stabilizing and grounding to the body. Originally they protect and strengthen the plants that produce them.

Ginger
Zingiber officinale

Pungent ginger root yields a warming and spicy essential oil. It can improve energy levels.

Plant profile: ginger is a key ingredient in the recipes of India and China. It is also used in Traditional Chinese Medicine for digestion and circulation problems. Ginger roots are dried before distillation, which means that the essential oil smells less pungent than the freshly chopped root.

Ginger has been used for centuries in Traditional Chinese Medicine to treat the digestion and circulation.

Safety information: no issues.

Fragrance profile: a dry, musty aroma, which is sharper and spicier as it evaporates, leaving a lingering sweetness.

Main uses: eases indigestion; warms and soothes aches and pains in muscles; improves poor circulation; improves energy.

Suggested blends: for indigestion, add 2 drops peppermint, 3 drops ginger, and 5 drops lemon to 4 teaspoons (20 ml) of carrier oil, then massage into the abdomen.

Aches and pains can be eased by taking a bath with 4 drops lavender and 2 drops ginger.

Improve circulation by massaging a blend of 6 drops black pepper and 4 drops ginger in 4 teaspoons (20 ml) carrier oil into the skin. You will notice the area becomes pink—this indicates improved circulation and is quite normal.

Vetiver is a very successful commercial crop in Indonesia as well as being a valuable essential oil.

Main uses: warms and relieves aches and pains, particularly backache; improves circulation; eases menstrual cramps; helps to ground and stabilize the emotions in cases of extreme stress.

Suggested blends: vetiver has a strong aroma, so use no more than 2 drops in a blend. For aches and pains and circulation, try 2 drops vetiver, 3 drops ginger, and 5 drops lavender in 4 teaspoons (20 ml) carrier oil for daily massage.

Ease menstrual cramps with a blend of 8 drops marjoram and 2 drops vetiver in 4 teaspoons (20 ml) carrier oil, massaged over the lower abdomen twice daily.

Emotional insecurity can be calmed by taking a bath with 1 drop vetiver, 1 drop neroli, and 3 drops lavender. Or add these oils to 2 teaspoons (10 ml) carrier oil and massage into the skin after your bath.

Massage an aching back with vetiver for relief from the pain. The warming scent is also very soothing to the mind and senses.

Vetiver

Vetiveria zizanoides

Plant profile: vetiver comes mainly from Indonesia, where it is known locally as, *akar wangi*. It is a tough tropical grass that is economically important to growers. The upper leaves can be woven into mats and fibers, while the aromatic roots are harvested for distillation. Vetiver is also grown on the island of Réunion in the Indian Ocean.

Safety information: no issues.

Fragrance profile: a very unusual deep, earthy, smoky aroma, heavy and warm.

Angelica

Angelica archangelica

The whole of the angelica plant is aromatic. However, it is the root of the plant that is used in the distillation of the essential oil.

Plant profile: a herb that has been highly regarded in Western herbal tradition since medieval times, angelica is now cultivated for essential oil extraction in countries including Germany and Hungary. The whole plant is aromatic. It grows to about 6 feet (2 meters) high and has dramatic spherical heads of tiny flowers. The pungent root has been used in herbal medicine for hundreds of years as a general cleanser and detoxifier.

Safety information: angelica essential oil is phototoxic. After any application to the skin, avoid direct exposure to strong sunlight or a sunbed for 12 hours. Angelica oil is best avoided in pregnancy.

Fragrance profile: sweet and aniseed-like, with a rich, warm, and spicy note that is released as it evaporates.

Main uses: eases muscular aches, soothes arthritic joints and rheumatic pains; eases indigestion problems and wind and improves poor appetite; an overall energy tonic and revitalizer, especially in the springtime.

Suggested blends: for muscular aches and pains, add 2 drops angelica, 2 drops vetiver, and 5 drops lavender to 4 teaspoons (20 ml) carrier oil and apply using gentle massage.

Digestion problems can be eased by blending 3 drops peppermint, 4 drops ginger, and 3 drops angelica in 4 teaspoons (20 ml) carrier oil for massage over the abdomen.

A "springtime blend" to help to energize and tone body and mind is 2 drops angelica, 3 drops juniper, and 5 drops grapefruit in 4 teaspoons (20 ml) carrier oil, to be massaged into the skin after a bath or shower.

The angelica plant produces beautiful spherical flowerheads. These are made up of thousands of tiny flowers. Angelica is now specifically cultivated for essential oil extraction.

Turmeric

Curcuma longa/Curcuma domestica

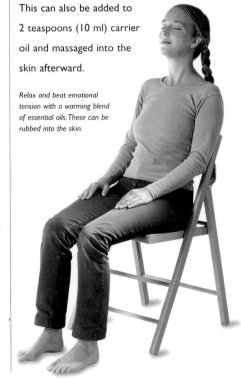

Yellow turmeric roots have many uses—they can be used as a cooking spice or an essential oil.

Plant profile: turmeric is a plant that looks very like ginger, with tall shoots and abundant elegant leaves, and is a member of the same botanical family. The highly aromatic roots are bright yellow and are used to color curries. The roots are cleaned and sun-dried before being ground as a spice or distilled for the oil. India, China, and Indonesia are the main producers.

Safety information: no issues.

Fragrance profile: dry, musty, and vegetable-like aroma; spicy and sweet as it evaporates.

Main uses: soothes and eases backache and muscular pains; improves circulation; tones and improves the digestion, easing stomach cramps and constipation. Very stabilizing and grounding to overwrought emotions; warms and re-energizes the body.

Suggested blends: for aches and pains, add 4 drops turmeric, 4 drops ginger, and 2 drops vetiver to 4 teaspoons (20 ml) carrier oil and apply using gentle massage.

Cramps and indigestion can be eased by blending 4 drops turmeric, 2 drops lemongrass, and 4 drops ginger in 4 teaspoons (20 ml) carrier oil, then massaging the blend into the abdomen.

For emotional tension, add 1 drop turmeric, 2 drops neroli, and 2 drops ginger to a warm bath and rest there for 20 minutes. This can also be added to 2 teaspoons (10 ml) carrier oil and massaged into the skin afterward.

Relax and beat emotional tension with a warming blend of essential oils. These can be rubbed into the skin.

Wood Oils

These oils are found in the aromatic heartwood in the center of tree trunks and branches. They are at the core of the growing, spreading height of the tree. The energy of these oils is more expansive, encouraging deep breathing.

Sandalwood
Santalum album

Plant profile: the best-quality sandalwood comes from the Mysore region of India near Bangalore. It takes approximately 30 years for the wood to mature to its full aromatic potential, so planting and harvesting is carefully rotated and controlled. The wood is used in the distillation of sandalwood oil. It is also powdered for making incense sticks and cosmetics, and can be carved into statues and boxes.

Safety information: no issues.

Fragrance profile: this beautiful oil should be thick and pale golden, with a subtle aroma at first, deepening to a rich, woody, spicy, sweet fragrance as it evaporates.

Main uses: eases tight chesty coughs, colds, sore throats; soothes dry chapped skin and improves the texture of all skin types; eases depression, anxiety, and feelings of panic.

Suggested blends: for coughs, add 3 drops sandalwood, 3 drops cedarwood, and 4 drops lemon to 4 teaspoons (20 ml) carrier oil and massage gently over the chest area.

A rejuvenating skincare blend is 6 drops sandalwood, 2 drops patchouli, and 2 drops rose in 4 teaspoons (20 ml) jojoba oil, massaged into the face at night.

For anxiety or depression, add 3 drops sandalwood and 2 drops orange to a warm bath and rest for 20 minutes. Add the same oils to 2 teaspoons (10 ml) carrier oil and massage into the skin afterward.

Sandalwood brings a state of peace and calm to body and mind. It is also good for use on sensitive skins.

Atlas Cedarwood

Cedrus atlantica

Plant profile: these tall, majestic cedar trees come from the Atlas mountains in Morocco. They stand over 100 feet (30 meters) in height with a sweeping, tentlike appearance, and a wonderful aroma floats around them thanks to the essential oil in the red heartwood. Cedar was used extensively by the ancient Egyptians in the manufacture of furniture and ships because of the wood's resistance to insects—as well as its beauty.

Safety information: no issues.

Fragrance profile: sharp and fresh with a sweet, woody, soft undertone.

The ancient Egyptians used fragrant cedarwood to make beautiful and aromatic furniture.

Cedarwood trees are huge and majestic, and are wonderfully aromatic too. The oil comes from the red heartwood.

Main uses: eases bronchitis, chest infections, coughs; soothes cracked skin, eczema, acne, and oily skin; assuages feelings of panic, calms and deepens the breath when under stress.

Suggested blends: Use 4 teaspoons (20 ml) carrier oil. For chest problems, add 3 drops cedarwood, 3 drops sandalwood, and 4 drops lemon and massage the chest. For cracked skin, add 3 drops cedarwood, 2 drops frankincense, and 5 drops lavender. For acne or oily skin, try 3 drops cedarwood, 2 drops tea tree, and 5 drops lavender in jojoba as a cleanser. For stress, vaporize 2 drops cedarwood and 3 drops lavender. Use these oils in 2 teaspoons (10 ml) carrier oil to massage the neck and shoulders.

Resin Oils

These sticky aromatic substances, the original incense ingredients, ooze out of the bark of certain trees and shrubs as a defense against injury. We too can use them to heal our skin.

Frankincense is the original "true incense" of antiquity and has been burned in places of religious worship for centuries.

Frankincense

Boswellia carterii var. *thurifera*

Plant profile: frankincense is a robust desert shrub with delicate leaves and whitish papery bark. The name actually means "true incense," and it has been burned in religious ceremonies since ancient times. The frankincense plantations of the pharaohs were seen as one of the most valuable commodities in Egypt and frankincense was used in the embalming process. Cuts were made in the bark to make the gum ooze out. It is still used for incense and distilled for the oil, mainly in Somalia and Oman.

Safety information: no issues.

Frankincense gum forms "tears" or granules. This oozes out of the bark of the frankincense shrub when it is cut.

Fragrance profile: fresh and sharp initially, deepening to woody, resiny with sweet notes.

Main uses: disinfects and heals cuts, wounds, eczema, and damaged skin; tones and rejuvenates all skin types, especially mature; eases chesty coughs or bronchitis; comforts anxiety and emotional stress.

Suggested blends: a good skin-healing blend is 4 drops frankincense, 2 drops lavender, and 4 drops cedarwood in 4 teaspoons (20 ml) carrier oil. Apply twice daily. A tonic for mature skin is 4 drops frankincense, 3 drops neroli, and 3 drops rose in 4 teaspoons (20 ml) jojoba oil. For chesty coughs, try an inhalation of 3 drops frankincense and 3 drops cedarwood. To ease emotional stress and help you relax, vaporize 3 drops frankincense and 4 drops grapefruit.

Myrrh

Commiphora myrrha

Plant profile: a thorny shrub, native to the arid climates of Somalia and Arabia, with papery bark and a reddish gum that oozes out when the bark is cracked or cut deliberately. Myrrh is soluble in water and has been used as a tonic for the teeth and gums since the time of Hippocrates (469–399 BCE), the father of Western medicine. Like frankincense, myrrh is prized for wound healing, and was used by the ancient Egyptians for embalming.

Myrrh gum is reddish-orange in color and was used in the embalming process in ancient Egypt.

Safety information: myrrh is best avoided during pregnancy.

Fragrance profile: a dry, sharp, and subtle aroma, which gradually deepens to reveal rich, sweet, and spicy notes.

Main uses: heals and disinfects deep cuts, wounds, chapped and cracked skin, eczema; cleans and disinfects the mouth, easing sore gums and mouth ulcers; relieves bronchitis, chesty coughs; comforts and calms highly anxious emotional states.

Suggested blends: Use 4 teaspoons (20 ml) carrier oil. To help damaged skin, add 3 drops myrrh, 4 drops tea tree, and 3 drops frankincense and apply 2–3 times daily. For chesty coughs, add 3 drops myrrh, 3 drops frankincense, and 4 drops cedarwood and massage the chest area, especially at night. For problems in the mouth, add 2 drops myrrh to a glass of water, then stir vigorously and use as a mouthwash (do not swallow). To de-stress, add 2 drops myrrh and 3 drops geranium to a bath—and relax.

Using myrrh as a mouthwash helps to keep teeth and gums healthy. Remember never to swallow any.

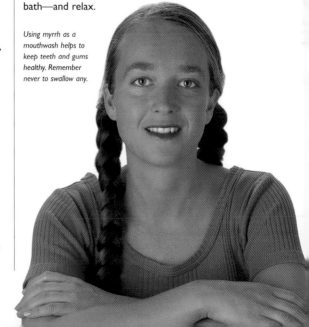

Leaf Oils

These oils are contained in the all-important leaves that manufacture the plant's food. They protect the leaf surface from damage by fungi and bacteria.

Marjoram

Origanum marjorana

French marjoram has a gentle woody aroma. The scent evaporates quite quickly.

Plant profile: this is the species otherwise known as "French marjoram," and not Spanish marjoram, which is a type of thyme. French marjoram has been a favorite herb for cooking and has been widely used for centuries. It is low-growing, with small aromatic leaves and tiny white flowers that appear in summer. Originally from Mediterranean regions, it will grow well in more northerly climates if kept sheltered and in a sunny spot. The essential oil comes from France.

Safety information: no issues.

Fragrance profile: a warm, woody aroma that somewhat resembles camphor, gradually becoming sweet and soft.

Main uses: helps muscular aches and pains, stiffness, and strains; eases menstrual cramps and mood swings; helps migraine, headaches, and nervous tension.

Suggested blends: Use 4 teaspoons (20 ml) carrier oil. For muscular aches, add 4 drops marjoram, 4 drops ginger, and 2 drops vetiver for massage. For menstrual symptoms, add 4 drops marjoram, 4 drops lavender, and 2 drops vetiver, then massage the abdomen.

For headaches and nervous tension, add 4 drops marjoram, 2 drops peppermint, and 4 drops lavender and then gently massage the forehead, neck, and shoulders.

Using essential oils like marjoram can help headaches and menstrual problems.

Peppermint

Mentha piperita

Peppermint is a strongly scented herb and grows very easily and quickly in the garden.

Plant profile: peppermint is a tall vigorous mint with a very invasive habit—ask any gardener! It spreads rapidly through tough root systems, and will displace other more tender herbs in a plot unless it is contained in some way. The square, erect stems support deep-green aromatic leaves and, if left untrimmed, the plant will produce tall heads of tiny white flowers. Peppermint essential oil comes mostly from the USA, and is used, in particular, to flavor toothpaste and chewing gum.

Safety information: if your skin is sensitive, use half the stated drops of peppermint in any blend due to the menthol content in the oil, which can act as an irritant.

Fragrance profile: pungent, fresh, zesty, and minty aroma with sweeter notes later.

Main uses: eases stomach cramps, indigestion, constipation, and nausea; helps muscular aches, stiffness, backache; eases headaches and migraine; clears the head and improves concentration.

Suggested blends: Use 4 teaspoons (20 ml) carrier oil. For indigestion symptoms, add 2 drops peppermint, 4 drops ginger, and 4 drops cardamom and massage the abdomen.

For aches and pains, add 2 drops peppermint, 4 drops rosemary, and 4 drops black pepper, and massage daily. To ease headaches, add 2 drops peppermint and 3 drops lavender to 2 teaspoons (10 ml) carrier oil and massage onto the forehead and neck.

For clearing the mind, vaporize 2 drops peppermint and 3 drops lemon.

Vaporizing peppermint essential oil in the office can clear your head and kick-start the mind.

Rosemary

Rosmarinus officinalis

Rosemary is an evergreen herb with a bracing aroma. It is used in cooking as well as aromatherapy.

Plant profile: the name "rosemary" means "rose of the sea," a reference to the original habitat of the plant on the dry, sandy coastline of the Mediterranean Sea. Even today, the best pungent oil comes from Spain or North Africa; the hotter and drier the climate, the better the aroma. Rosemary oil smells quite similar to eucalyptus because they have a fragrant ingredient in common: eucalyptol.

Safety information: rosemary is not advised for people with high blood pressure, as it is a stimulating oil. It should also be avoided by people who suffer from epilepsy.

Fragrance profile: strong, camphoraceous, fresh, and herbal aroma with a definite eucalyptus tone.

Main uses: eases muscular aches and pains, backache, poor circulation; stimulates the scalp and eases dandruff; clears the breathing in colds, influenza, or sinusitis; stimulates the mind and wakes up the brain.

Suggested blends: for aches and pains and for poor circulation, try using 4 drops rosemary, 2 drops lemongrass, and 4 drops nutmeg in 4 teaspoons (20 ml) carrier oil.

For a hair and scalp tonic, try adding 5 drops rosemary and 5 drops tea tree to 4 teaspoons (20 ml) of unfragranced shampoo and then washing your hair as normal.

For easier breathing when suffering from colds or influenza, add 3 drops rosemary and 3 drops tea tree to a bowl of nearly boiling water and inhale the vapor for 20 minutes. To help stimulate the mind, vaporize 3 drops rosemary and 3 drops peppermint.

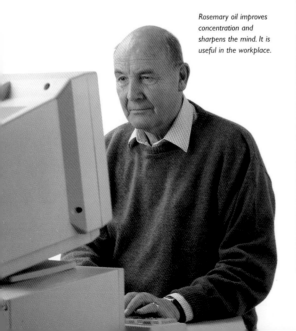

Rosemary oil improves concentration and sharpens the mind. It is useful in the workplace.

Cypress

Cupressus sempervivens

Plant profile: tall, evergreen cypress trees are an elegant feature of the landscape in Italy, France, Corsica, Sardinia, Spain, and Portugal. The Latin name *sempervivens* means "ever living," a reference to the long life of the species. They are often planted near dwellings or near churches to signify eternal life. The oil comes from the young twigs and leaves, which are highly aromatic. Distillation takes place mostly in France or Spain.

Safety information: no issues.

Fragrance profile: earthy, smoky, and green with camphoraceous and sweet notes.

Main uses: clears oily skin and blocked pores; improves lymphatic drainage and cellulite; eases spasmodic coughs and bronchitis; soothes fraught emotions.

The tall dark shapes of cypress trees stand out clearly in a Mediterranean landscape.

Suggested blends: oily skin can be treated daily using 3 drops cypress, 3 drops tea tree, and 4 drops grapefruit in 4 teaspoons (20 ml) jojoba oil to cleanse and soothe the skin.

To counter cellulite, try using 4 drops cypress, 4 drops grapefruit, and 2 drops juniper in 4 teaspoons (20 ml) carrier oil for a vigorous daily massage of the affected areas.

To ease spasmodic coughs, do an inhalation with 3 drops cypress and 2 drops cedarwood twice daily; these oils can also be added to 2 teaspoons (10 ml) carrier oil and massaged into the chest.

If your emotions are overstretched or you are stressed, take a soothing bath with 3 drops cypress and 3 drops lavender and relax deeply.

Cypress essential oil is useful as a soothing skin treatment for an oily or blemished complexion.

Petitgrain (orange leaf)

Citrus aurantium var. *amara*

Petitgrain is one of three oils taken from the bitter orange tree. Unlike most citrus oils, petitgrain is not phototoxic.

Plant profile: petitgrain is one of three essential oils produced by the bitter orange tree. The leaves of the orange tree contain tiny sacs of essential oil, which are visible (like grains) to the naked eye when a leaf is held up to the sun—the French name of the oil means "little grain." The oil is an original ingredient of eau de cologne, popular since the eighteenth century. Most petitgrain oil comes from France or Paraguay.

Safety information: no issues. (Unlike orange, this oil is not phototoxic.)

Fragrance profile: a green, fresh, bittersweet aroma with a hint of citrus.

Main uses: tones, refreshes, and balances oily and combination skins; eases stomach cramps, indigestion, and wind; calms and soothes the mind, releasing tension and nervous exhaustion.

Suggested blends: for oily/combination skin, add 4 drops petitgrain, 2 drops patchouli, and 4 drops lavender to 4 teaspoons (20 ml) jojoba oil and use as a cleanser and skin-soother twice a day.

To ease stomach cramps, add 4 drops petitgrain, 2 drops peppermint, and 4 drops roman chamomile to 4 teaspoons (20 ml) carrier oil and massage the abdomen (half the dose of drops in 4 teaspoons (20 ml) carrier can be used on children).

To relieve stress and calm the nerves, add 3 drops petitgrain and 3 drops sandalwood to a warm bath and relax.

Petitgrain is a fragrance note that can be found in many old-fashioned colognes.

Patchouli

Pogostemon patchouli

Patchouli leaves are soft, velvety, and highly aromatic. The leaves are used in India to protect textiles from moths.

Plant profile: patchouli comes from India in the form of a thick, golden-brown essential oil with a very pronounced aroma. The leaves of the patchouli plant have a velvety texture thanks to thousands of tiny hairs on the surface. These contain microscopic sacs of essential oil, so that when you rub the leaf, the aroma is very strong on your fingers. Patchouli leaves are used to protect cloth from moths in India, and the oil is regarded as an insect repellent. It is also traditionally used in India as a skin conditioner and antiseptic.

Safety information: no issues.

Fragrance profile: a rich, velvety, musky aroma that develops spicy, earthy, and sweet tones with time.

Main uses: helps to soothe cracked, chapped, and dry skin and eczema; improves the complexion of mature and dry skins; increases sexual energy and helps to enhance sensuality.

Suggested blends: for dry, damaged, or cracked skin, try creating a massage blend of 3 drops patchouli, 3 drops cedarwood, and 4 drops roman chamomile in 4 teaspoons (20 ml) jojoba oil and apply as needed.

To improve the complexion, add 3 drops patchouli, 4 drops frankincense, and 3 drops sandalwood to 4 teaspoons (20 ml) carrier oil and massage into the face, especially at night (this is appropriate for both men and women).

For a sensual massage blend, add 3 drops patchouli, 2 drops rose, and 5 drops orange to 4 teaspoons (20 ml) carrier oil.

Patchouli makes a wonderful relaxing and sensual blend. The essential oil can increase and enhance sexual energy.

Eucalyptus
Eucalyptus globulus

Plant profile: there are more than 700 species of eucalyptus. In aromatherapy, several eucalyptus oils are used, of which *Eucalyptus globulus* is the most common. This evergreen tree from Australia can grow to a height of up to 300 feet (90 meters) when mature. The aromatic leaves are bluish-green on the upper surface and paler underneath. The leaves and the essential oil have been widely used as a household remedy in Australia from the days of the Aborigines to treat fevers, respiratory conditions, and skin infections.

Safety information: must not be swallowed —cases of severe internal poisoning have occurred. Safe on the skin or as an inhalation.

The eucalyptus tree is native to Australia and is an attractive evergreen with blue-green foliage.

Fragrance profile: extremely fresh and bracing, with woodier tones later.

Main uses: clears colds, blocked noses, sinusitis, chest infections; soothes burns, cuts, wounds, and insect bites; eases muscular pains; improves circulation; improves concentration.

Suggested blends: for colds and chest problems, use 2 drops eucalyptus and 3 drops tea tree in an inhalation twice daily. Add this combination of oils to 2 teaspoons (10 ml) carrier oil and massage into the chest area.

Use 4 teaspoons (20 ml) carrier oil. For damaged skin, add 2 drops eucalyptus, 3 drops tea tree, and 5 drops lavender, then apply twice daily.

For muscle pains, add 3 drops eucalyptus, 4 drops rosemary, and 3 drops ginger, and use for massage. To improve concentration, vaporize 3 drops eucalyptus and 3 drops rosemary.

Eucalyptus is one of the best oils to use for inhalations and for clearing catarrh.

Tea tree essential oil is taken from the leaves of the tree and is very pungent and antiseptic.

Tea Tree

Melaleuca alternifolia

Plant profile: tea tree is native to Australia, where it has long been used by the aboriginal people as an antiseptic. The name "tea tree" refers to the practice of drinking an infusion of the leaves as a healing herbal drink, first observed by the sailors on Captain Cook's ship in the eighteenth century. Production of the oil is now a huge commercial enterprise with a whole host of tea tree products available on the market, from toothpaste to foot powder. It is one of the most antiseptic plants ever discovered.

Tea tree can help to treat the symptoms of influenza. Inhale the oil from a tissue whenever necessary.

Safety information: safe to use neat on the skin (2 drops on an absorbent cotton pad applied directly to the affected area) except on individuals with sensitive or allergy-prone skin, for whom it must be diluted in carrier oil.

Fragrance profile: medicinal, green, camphoraceous aroma, pungent and strong.

Main uses: clears skin infections and acne; heals wounds and cuts; soothes insect bites; clears athlete's foot; helps influenza, colds, bronchitis; boosts general immunity.

Suggested blends: for skin infections, add 4 drops tea tree, 3 drops sandalwood, and 3 drops lavender to 4 teaspoons (20 ml) carrier oil and apply as necessary. For chest problems, use an inhalation of 3 drops tea tree and 3 drops lemon twice daily. To boost immunity, add 2 drops tea tree, 2 drops bergamot, and 1 drop black pepper to a warm bath. Add these same oils to 2 teaspoons (10 ml) carrier oil and massage the upper chest area daily during an episode of influenza.

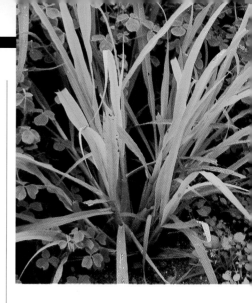

Lemongrass
Cymbopogon citratus

Plant profile: lemongrass is an aromatic tropical grass from India. It is well known as a flavoring ingredient in Indian and Thai cooking. In India, the grass is used in traditional medicine to help reduce fevers and kill infections, and also as an insect repellent. The leaves are chopped just above ground level and, as with all grasses, new shoots are then produced very quickly.

Lemongrass is a vigorous and aromatic tropical plant. It should always be diluted—even in blends for the bath.

Safety information: the oil is regarded as a potential irritant to already sensitive or allergic skin and is not advised for infants and young children. It should always be diluted in a carrier, even in bath blends.

Fragrance profile: a very strong, "lemon sherbet" aroma that is zesty and sweet with a slightly heavy undertone.

Main uses: eases muscular aches, pains, and stiffness; eases stomach cramps, indigestion, and constipation; lifts depression or anxiety and improves the mood.

Suggested blends: for muscular aches, add 2 drops lemongrass, 3 drops rosemary, and 5 drops cardamom to 4 teaspoons (20 ml) carrier oil to massage the specific areas.

For stomach cramps or constipation, add 2 drops lemongrass, 4 drops coriander, and 4 drops nutmeg to 4 teaspoons (20 ml) carrier oil and massage the abdomen twice daily.

To improve mood and combat stress, add 2 drops lemongrass, 2 drops rose, and 6 drops frankincense to 4 teaspoons (20 ml) carrier oil.

Lemongrass is a key flavoring in most Thai dishes. Its zesty character can really lift a dish.

Palmarosa
Cymbopogon martini

Aromatic palmarosa is another grass grown in India. It has a similar fragrance to rose oil.

Plant profile: palmarosa is another aromatic grass from India, this time with a sweet smell and an altogether milder effect when used. In the past, it has often been used to adulterate or dilute pure rose oil, because the fragrance is somewhat similar and the grass is produced much more cheaply and in far larger quantities than rose. Palmarosa has a long-lasting aroma, which makes it a popular cosmetic ingredient in soaps, toiletries, and perfumes.

Safety information: no issues.

Fragrance profile: a long-lasting, sweet, and roselike aroma, which is soft and gentle with slightly lemony tones.

Main uses: soothes and calms irritated skin, acne, eczema, dermatitis; improves the facial complexion in all skin types, especially combination and mature; soothes cystitis and clears urinary tract infections; calms and de-stresses the nerves.

Suggested blends: Use 4 teaspoons (20 ml) carrier oil. For sensitive or irritated skin, add 3 drops palmarosa and 2 drops roman chamomile (note the low dilution) and apply as needed. To balance and rejuvenate the complexion, add 4 drops palmarosa, 3 drops frankincense, and 3 drops sandalwood and massage the face, especially at night. To uplift your mood, add 3 drops palmarosa, 4 drops grapefruit, and 3 drops orange, for an exotic and soft massage blend. For cystitis or urinary problems, add 3 drops palmarosa and 3 drops sandalwood to a warm bath to soothe the area.

Palmarosa oil cares for and nurtures all skin types. It also de-stresses overstretched nerves.

wer Oils

These are some of the most exquisite fragrances you will encounter. Captured from the petals, they are the unique aromatic signal of that plant.

Lavender
Lavandula angustifolia

Plant profile: lavender oil is now widely produced in the UK, southern France, Tasmania, New Zealand, and Bulgaria. Purple lavender fields make one of the most wonderful aromatic landscapes, filled with bees and butterflies busily enjoying the magnificent supply of pollen. Lavender oils vary in fragrance according to the altitude where they are produced—high altitude oils have sharper and fresher aromas, and low altitude ones are sweeter and softer.

Safety information: no issues. Lavender can be used neat (2 drops on an absorbent cotton pad applied directly to the affected area).

Fragrance profile: mainly soft, sweet, and floral with camphoraceous and pungent notes.

Main uses: soothes cuts, burns, wounds, insect bites, sore skin; eases headaches, migraine, and muscular aches and tension; soothes chesty spasmodic coughs; helps insomnia, nervous tension, and anxiety; useful for both adults and children.

Suggested blends: for skin problems, add 4 drops lavender, 3 drops tea tree, and 3 drops roman chamomile to 4 teaspoons (20 ml) carrier oil and massage into the affected area.

Ease headaches by adding 3 drops lavender to 1 teaspoon (5 ml) carrier oil and massaging the forehead and neck to provide relief.

To relieve coughs, an inhalation with 4 drops lavender and 3 drops cedarwood done twice daily can often be helpful.

To ease insomnia, vaporize 3 drops lavender and 3 drops orange to help you fall asleep.

Lavender fields are vibrantly purple and wonderfully aromatic. Bees and butterflies love visiting the plants that grow here.

Geranium

Pelargonium graveolens

The leaves of this geranium release a strong rosy aroma.

Plant profile:

this is a tropical geranium with velvety, frilly leaves. Rubbing the tiny surface hairs releases a strong, rosy aroma onto your fingers. The geranium grows as a shrub up to 3 feet (1 meter) in height and has pinkish flowers. The essential oil has a powerful floral aroma. The island of Réunion in the Indian Ocean produces the best-quality oil. Chinese and Egyptian geranium oils are also available but have a much heavier fragrance.

Safety information:

no issues.

Fragrance profile:

rosy, sweet, and strong, with a hint of lemon and fresh green notes.

Main uses: soothes cracked and inflamed skin, eczema, dermatitis, acne, and congested or oily skin; eases premenstrual symptoms such as lack of energy, bloatedness, and fluid retention; soothes mood swings and helps to balance hormonally related emotional upsets.

Suggested blends: for skin problems, add 3 drops geranium, 3 drops sandalwood, and 4 drops lavender to 4 teaspoons (20 ml) carrier oil and apply to the area as needed.

To ease premenstrual symptoms, try adding 2 drops geranium and 3 drops petitgrain to a warm bath. You can also use the same combination of oils in 2 teaspoons (10 ml) carrier oil for an uplifting massage afterward.

To help balance mood swings, add 3 drops geranium, 3 drops lemon, and 4 drops orange to 4 teaspoons (20 ml) carrier oil and massage into your skin for a floral and citrus uplift.

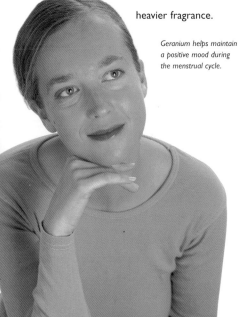

Geranium helps maintain a positive mood during the menstrual cycle.

Ylang Ylang

Cananga odorata

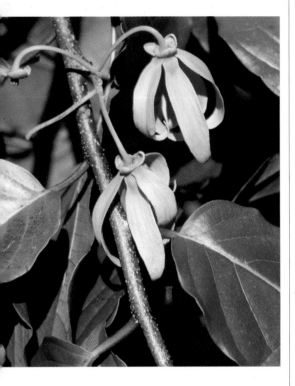

Ylang ylang flowers are beautiful exotic blooms, which yield large amounts of deeply scented essential oil.

Plant profile: from Madagascar, an island off the coast of East Africa, comes the "flower of flowers"—ylang ylang. Beautiful, lush, golden-yellow flowers with velvety petals produce a wonderful oil very similar to jasmine. There is such a high content of fragrance in the flowers that the essential oil can be drawn off three times during the process of distillation, offering three grades of essential oil. The first collection of oil is known as the "perfume" grade and is the best quality.

Safety information: no major issues. Some individuals find the strong floral aroma brings on a headache.

Fragrance profile: sharp and sweet, becoming deeply floral, jasmine-like, heady, and soft with time.

Main uses: tones oily and combination skins; reduces panic attacks and stress-related anxiety symptoms; soothes and calms emotional stress and overstretched nerves.

Suggested blends: to tone oily skin, add 2 drops ylang ylang, 3 drops sandalwood, and 5 drops frankincense to 4 teaspoons (20 ml) jojoba oil and use as a cleanser and skin-soother twice daily.

For panic and anxiety attacks, add 2 drops ylang ylang and 3 drops lavender to a warm bath, and add the same combination of oils to 2 teaspoons (10 ml) carrier oil for a relaxing neck and shoulder massage afterward.

To soothe the nerves and ease anxiety, add 2 drops ylang ylang, 2 drops patchouli, and 5 drops orange to 4 teaspoons (20 ml) carrier oil and massage your body gently.

Rose

Rosa damascena

Plant profile: costly and labor-intensive to produce, rose is one of the most beautiful of all essential oils. The little damask rose from Kazanlik in Bulgaria produces the finest quality rose oil, although Turkish, Moroccan, and Russian rose oils are also excellent. Rose "otto" is simply distilled rose oil—between 50 and 100 blooms are needed per drop. An "absolute" of rose, chemically extracted, is also available at a lower cost. Look out for pure rose oil already diluted in jojoba as a more affordable and still effective way to use this oil.

Safety information: no issues.

Fragrance profile: honey-sweet, slightly lemony, and soft, with richness and depth.

The damask rose has a uniquely glorious aroma. It is one of the most costly oils to produce but is worth every drop.

Main uses: tones and rejuvenates all skin types, especially dry, sensitive, and mature; eases premenstrual and menopausal symptoms; helps release feelings of grief and separation, restoring the heart.

Suggested blends: to tone the skin, add 2 drops rose, 4 drops frankincense, and 4 drops sandalwood to 4 teaspoons (20 ml) jojoba oil (halve the number of drops for sensitive skin). For premenstrual or menopausal symptoms, add 4 drops rose, 3 drops neroli, and 3 drops mandarin to 4 teaspoons (20 ml) carrier oil and massage into the body. To ease grief, add 2 drops rose and 3 drops orange to a bath. Use the same combination in 2 teaspoons (10 ml) carrier oil for a massage afterward.

Pure rose oil trickled into a bath releases an amazing fragrance, which can relieve stress almost instantly.

ו Chamomile

ɔbilis

Plant profile: the name "chamomile" is originally from the Greek *kamaimelon,* meaning "ground apple." This derives from the fact that the plant is low-growing and smells strongly of apples. In its non-flowering variety, this species of chamomile is often used to make a fragrant lawn. The flowers, however, are required for distillation.

The oil has a pale blue color due to the presence of a substance called "azulene," which has anti-inflammatory properties. The oil is now cultivated successfully in the UK.

Safety information: no issues.

Fragrance profile: fruity (apple-like), sweet, fresh, and soft.

Main uses: soothes cuts, burns, sore, dry skin, diaper rash; eases menstrual cramps, premenstrual low energy, and tension; soothes headaches, migraine; helps insomnia, nervous exhaustion, tension, restlessness, and stress-related problems.

The yellow flowers and leaves of roman chamomile are very aromatic.

Suggested blends: Use 4 teaspoons (20 ml) carrier oil. For skin problems, add 3 drops roman chamomile, 4 drops lavender, and 3 drops palmarosa and apply as necessary; for baby diaper rash, use 1 drop only of chamomile for an extremely gentle application.

For menstrual symptoms, add 3 drops roman chamomile and 2 drops marjoram to a warm bath, then add this blend of oils to 2 teaspoons (10 ml) carrier oil and massage the lower abdomen.

For insomnia and restlessness, try vaporizing 3 drops roman chamomile and 3 drops lavender in the bedroom before turning in for the night.

Babies and younger children respond well to the fragrance of roman chamomile essential oil.

Neroli (orange blossom)

Citrus aurantium var. amara

Plant profile: the essential oil from orange blossom is named after princess Neroli, an Italian noblewoman of the Renaissance period who perfumed her gloves with Neroli flowers. The oil has an enchanting aroma, and is costly and labor-intensive to produce, as the fragrant white flowers of the bitter orange tree have to be picked by hand. Neroli essential oil is mostly distilled in France and Morocco. Look out for pure neroli diluted in jojoba from quality essential oil ranges, as this is a more affordable way of trying this fragrance.

Safety information: no issues.

Fragrance profile: creamy-sweet, citrusy, rich, and soft with green undertones.

Main uses: tones and rejuvenates the complexion, especially dry, mature, or undernourished skins; helps scar tissue, wounds, and cuts; eases nervous indigestion and irritable bowel symptoms; helps calm panic, shock, and sudden emotional upsets.

Suggested blends: for skincare, add 3 drops neroli, 4 drops frankincense, and 3 drops

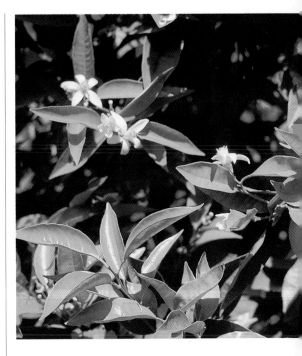

Each orange blossom has to be picked by hand, making neroli— along with rose—one of the more expensive essential oils.

patchouli to 4 teaspoons (20 ml) jojoba for a nourishing facial massage oil.

To heal damaged skin, add 3 drops neroli, 4 drops lavender, and 4 drops myrrh to 4 teaspoons (20 ml) carrier oil and apply to the area twice daily. For nervous indigestion, add 4 drops neroli, 3 drops peppermint, and 3 drops ginger to 4 teaspoons (20 ml) carrier oil for gentle abdominal massage as necessary.

To help shock and panic, simply place 2 drops neroli on a tissue and inhale the fragrance until calm is restored.

Berry and Seed Oils

These are aromatic packages of pungent fragrance, often designed to attract animals and birds. They ingest the seeds and then eventually release them into the earth, helping plant reproduction.

Nutmeg
Myristica fragrans

Aromatic nutmegs have a spicy, cheering fragrance. They can be used in cakes and cookies to give a distinctive flavor.

Plant profile: the nutmeg tree grows in Indonesia and Sri Lanka. The fruits are covered with a layer called mace, which is removed before processing. The highly aromatic nutmegs are steam-distilled to give a fragrant essential oil. In Western herbal tradition, nutmegs were prized for their digestive tonic and muscle-warming properties. In medieval times they were so valuable they were kept locked away.

Safety information: a strong oil, so should be used in moderation.

Fragrance profile: warm, sharp, spicy, and sweet with a distinctive softness later.

Main uses: eases muscular aches and pains, arthritic pain, and cold extremities; soothes and calms indigestion, stomach cramps, nausea; helps to re-energize the body after illness, speeding convalescence, uplifting the spirits, and restoring the circulation.

Suggested blends: Use 4 teaspoons (20 ml) carrier oil. For aches and pains, add 2 drops nutmeg, 4 drops cardamom, and 4 drops grapefruit, and massage into the affected area. To soothe the digestion, add 2 drops nutmeg, 4 drops peppermint, and 4 drops ginger for an abdominal massage. As a restoring tonic, add 1 drop nutmeg, 2 drops black pepper, and 2 drops orange to a warm bath and relax in the water. Add the same oils to 2 teaspoons (10 ml) carrier oil and massage into the skin afterward.

Blends made using nutmeg can ease muscular cramps.

Black Pepper

Piper nigrum

Plant profile: this plant is a trailing vinelike climber with lovely, heart-shaped, dark green leaves and clusters of white flowers that become the berries—or peppercorns. These turn from red to black as they mature (white pepper has had the outer layer removed). Black peppercorns are steam-distilled to yield the essential oil. The tropical plant is native to India, and the oil is produced there as well as in Indonesia and Malaysia.

Safety information: no issues.

Fragrance profile: warm, musty, sharp, and spicy, with heavier sweet notes later.

Main uses: warms and stimulates blood circulation; helps to ease aches and pains; soothes indigestion, stomach cramps, and constipation; strengthens the immune system, especially against influenza.

Suggested blends: to help stimulate poor or sluggish circulation, add 4 drops black pepper, 2 drops lemongrass, and 4 drops cardamom to 4 teaspoons (20 ml) carrier oil and massage into the affected area as needed.

Black peppercorns yield a warm and pungent oil, which has a very spicy aroma. Black pepper essential oil can boost the immune system and ease indigestion.

To ease indigestion or constipation, add 3 drops black pepper, 3 drops peppermint, and 4 drops neroli to 4 teaspoons (20 ml) carrier oil and massage the abdomen twice daily.

To boost the immune system, add 1 drop black pepper, 2 drops tea tree, and 2 drops bergamot to an evening bath and soak for at least 20 minutes. Add these oils to 4 teaspoons (20 ml) carrier oil and massage the chest area afterward.

Poor circulation can be helped by vigorously massaging the area in question with the pepper blend.

Cardamom

Elettaria cardamomum

Essential oils like cardamom improve the mood and warm the affected areas. Cardamom is a good energy tonic too.

Plant profile: a member of the same plant family as ginger, cardamom produces aromatic flowers that turn into little seed pods filled with tiny black seeds. The pods are traditionally chewed in India to sweeten the breath after eating spicy food, and the wonderful aroma of cardamom is also used to flavor Indian ice cream and confectionery. Cardamom is commonly used in Eastern medicinal traditions as a lung tonic and immunity-boosting plant remedy.

Safety information: no issues.

Fragrance profile: warm, fruity, sweet, and spicy with a mouthwatering pungent freshness.

Main uses: soothes and opens the chest, helping breathing and congestion; warms and soothes stomach cramps and indigestion; uplifts the mind and gives a positive feeling when energy is low.

Suggested blends: to improve breathing, add 3 drops cardamom and 2 drops cedarwood to nearly boiling water and inhale the vapor, repeating twice daily; add the same oils to 2 teaspoons (10 ml) carrier oil and massage the chest area afterward.

To ease digestion problems, massage the abdomen twice daily with 3 drops cardamom, 3 drops coriander, and 4 drops orange in 4 teaspoons (20 ml) carrier oil.

As a tonic to raise low spirits, add 3 drops cardamom and 2 drops mandarin to a warm bath and relax in the water. Add the same oils to 2 teaspoons (10 ml) carrier oil and massage into the skin afterward.

May Chang

Litsea cubeba

May chang has berries that smell like lemon sherbet! It is not a suitable oil for babies and young children.

Plant profile: a tree from China with delicate leaves and little whitish-yellow flowers that become highly lemon-scented tiny fruits. The oil from the berries of the may chang tree is used a great deal in China as a mood enhancer and as a tonic to the heart; it calms and regulates the heart rhythm when used in massage. It is similar to lemongrass, but has a much lighter and sweeter fragrance.

Fresh lemony scents, such as may chang, have a cheering effect on the body and mind and can help ease mood swings.

Safety information: avoid using this oil on sensitive or damaged skin. It is not suitable for babies or children. Always dilute this oil, even if you are using it in the bath.

Fragrance profile: soft, sweet, and fruity with a strong "lemon sherbet" aroma that is zesty and mouthwatering.

Main uses: eases muscular aches and pains, strains, and backache; eases panic or stress attacks; uplifts depression and anxiety, mood swings, and tearfulness.

Suggested blends: for aches and pains, add 2 drops may chang, 4 drops juniper, and 4 drops lavender and massage affected areas.

Panic and stress attacks can be eased by simply placing 2 drops may chang on a tissue and inhaling the aroma for a few minutes. Add 2 drops may chang and 3 drops neroli to a warm bath and relax in the water to recover.

Uplift moods and ease depression by a massage with a blend of 2 drops may chang, 2 drops rose, and 6 drops frankincense in 4 teaspoons (20 ml) carrier oil.

Juniper

Juniperus communis

Blue-black juniper berries are sharp and pungently scented. They take up to two years to turn black.

Plant profile: juniper is a vigorous shrub with dark green spiky leaves. The essential oil comes mainly from Germany, where the plant grows well, and also from parts of Croatia. The berries on the juniper bush take up to two years to turn black and produce the best-quality oil. Juniper is also used in making gin, and in northern European cooking it is used to give pungent flavor to root vegetables. In herbal medicine, juniper is considered to be a strong diuretic and internal cleanser.

Safety information: this is best avoided during pregnancy, and also by people with any serious kidney complaints.

Fragrance profile: pungent, peppery, and camphoraceous, with sweeter, softer notes developing later.

Main uses: helps to clear lymphatic congestion and detoxify the system; opens the chest and eases breathing in respiratory complaints; freshens the mind and helps improve concentration.

Suggested blends: to help detoxify, add 2 drops juniper, 2 drops angelica, and 6 drops grapefruit to 4 teaspoons (20 ml) carrier oil for a vigorous daily massage to affected areas of the body.

To help respiratory complaints, add 2 drops juniper and 3 drops eucalyptus to a bowl of nearly boiling water and inhale the vapors. Do this twice daily. To help concentration, vaporize 3 drops juniper and 3 drops lemon in a room; this also helps to clear the atmosphere and neutralize any stale or unpleasant odors.

Massage blends with juniper can help improve areas of poor circulation in the legs. A vigorous daily massage is recommended.

Coriander Seed

Coriandrum sativum

Coriander seeds are a pungent spice and are used frequently in Indian cuisine. The leaves are also used as a delicious garnish.

Plant profile: the coriander plant is a highly aromatic herb with deliciously flavored dark green leaves (cilantro). It is easy to grow and makes a pungent addition to salad greens and a wonderful garnish for Indian dishes. The coriander plant produces umbels— umbrella-like stalks topped with little white flowers that eventually turn to brownish-colored aromatic seeds. These are distilled to produce the essential oil in Eastern European countries, including Russia and Croatia.

Safety information: no issues.

Fragrance profile: woody, spicy, and sweet with a slight hint of musk.

Main uses: warms and soothes muscular stiffness and aching joints; helps build immunity, especially in the case of influenza; eases mental exhaustion and overstretched nerves.

Coriander is a herb widely used in cooking and herbalism. It has attractive heads of white flowers.

Suggested blends: to warm muscles, add 3 drops coriander, 3 drops black pepper, and 4 drops ginger to 4 teaspoons (20 ml) carrier oil; massage twice daily. To boost the immune system, add 2 drops coriander and 3 drops lemon to a bath; then add the same oils to 2 teaspoons (10 ml) carrier oil and massage into the chest area. To ease exhaustion, add 2 drops coriander, 1 drop neroli, and 2 drops lavender to a bath; add the same oils to 2 teaspoons (10 ml) carrier oil afterward for a massage. This routine can also help improve sleep quality.

Fruit Oils

These oils are packed into tiny fragrant globules in the rind of citrus fruit. Fresh and zesty, they are mouthwatering aromas, loved by adults and children.

Orange (sweet)
Citrus sinensis

Plant profile: most orange essential oil that is commercially available is from the sweet orange tree, which originated in China. The essential oil is expressed, or crushed out of the rind of the fruit. The bitter orange tree (*Citrus aurantium*) produces petitgrain and neroli essential oils.

Orange trees are covered with delicious-smelling leaves, flowers, and fruits. Orange essential oil is popular with young and old alike.

Safety information: very mildly phototoxic; avoid exposure to strong sunlight or a sunbed for 12 hours after skin application.

Fragrance profile: sweet, warm, fresh, and citrusy.

Main uses: soothes stomach cramps and indigestion (especially in children); rejuvenates congested and slack skin; uplifts depression, mood swings, anxiety, and emotional stress.

Suggested blends: for stomach problems, add 4 drops orange, 2 drops peppermint, and 4 drops ginger to 4 teaspoons (20 ml) carrier oil and massage the abdomen 2–3 times daily (halve the number of drops for children).

To rejuvenate tired skin, add 4 drops orange, 4 drops frankincense, and 2 drops cypress to 4 teaspoons (20 ml) jojoba. For anxiety, add 2 drops orange, 1 drop rose, and 2 drops sandalwood to a bath; use this blend in 2 teaspoons (10 ml) carrier oil for massage.

Children particularly love the sweet soft aroma of orange essential oil. It is a popular festive smell!

Lemon

Citrus limonum

Lemon rind is packed full of fres
zesty essential oil. It is a good oil
concentration and sharpen the n

Plant profile: the finest essential oil of lemon is considered to come from trees grown in Sicily, although the fruit is also cultivated in California, Florida, and Israel. The evergreen tree is thorny and has shiny, dark green, aromatic leaves that produce an essential oil called *petitgrain citronnier.* The fragrant flowers turn into the fruit, which when ripe are a warm golden yellow. Essential oil of lemon is expressed, or squeezed out of the peel of the fruit.

Safety information: mildly phototoxic; avoid any exposure to strong sunlight or a sunbed for at least 12 hours after application of the oil to the skin.

Fragrance profile: green, citrusy, and fresh, zesty, and bright; softer and more sherbety tones develop with time.

Main uses: helps build immunity against colds, influenza, and other viral infections; detoxifies the system and assists lymphatic drainage; freshens the mind and helps to improve concentration.

Lemon trees grow all over the Mediterranean, and particularly in Sicily. They are a wonderful sight in the summer.

Suggested blends: to help boost the immune system, vaporize 3 drops lemon and 2 drops tea tree to disinfect the air; add the same oils to 2 teaspoons (10 ml) carrier oil to massage the chest area twice daily.

To help detoxify the body, add 4 drops lemon, 2 drops angelica, and 4 drops juniper to 4 teaspoons (20 ml) carrier oil and massage the legs and other affected areas twice daily.

To assist concentration and improve alertness, add 3 drops lemon and 3 drops rosemary to a vaporizer; this is especially helpful when studying.

Mandarin

Citrus reticulata

Mandarin has a soft, bittersweet citrus aroma. The essential oil is used in soaps and cosmetics.

Plant profile: this small citrus tree is evergreen and its fruit has an immediate association with festive celebrations. The fruit and the expressed oil are produced mainly in Brazil, Spain, and Italy. Because it is so mild and pleasant, mandarin is used as a flavoring in many confectionery items, liqueurs, and soft drinks, as well as in soaps, toiletries, and perfumes. It is a favorite with children.

Safety information: very mildly phototoxic; avoid exposure to strong sunlight or a sunbed for 12 hours after application to the skin.

Fragrance profile: fresh, pungent, and sweet with a bright citrus zest; softer and more floral tones developing with time.

Main uses: clears congested and oily skin; soothes stomach cramps and nervous indigestion (especially in children); eases insomnia, restless sleep, and troubled dreams.

Suggested blends: for oily skin, add 4 drops mandarin, 3 drops cypress, and 3 drops juniper to 4 teaspoons (20 ml) jojoba oil and use as a cleanser and skin-soother at night.

To ease digestion problems, add 4 drops mandarin, 4 drops lavender, and 2 drops roman chamomile to 4 teaspoons (20 ml) carrier oil and gently massage the abdomen twice daily (halve the number of drops for children).

To help induce restful sleep, add 3 drops mandarin and 3 drops lavender to a vaporizer.

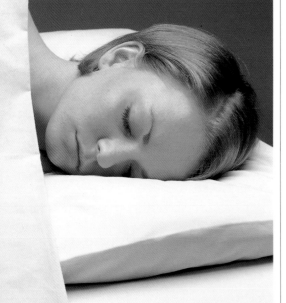

Vaporizing mandarin essential oil at night helps to improve sleep and ease any lingering anxiety.

Grapefruit

Citrus x paradisi

The large golden grapefruit produc different aroma from other citrus f

Plant profile: grapefruit is a hybrid which may have been derived from an old variety of fruit called the shaddock. It is now cultivated extensively in Florida in its familiar golden and pink-fleshed varieties. The essential oil is expressed from the peel, and grapefruit has an aroma quite different from its citrus relatives, thanks to the presence of sharp bitter constituents that give it freshness and zest.

Safety information: mildly phototoxic; avoid exposure to strong sunlight or a sunbed for 12 hours after application to the skin.

Fragrance profile: green, bittersweet, zesty, and fresh, with a soft, powdery afternote.

Main uses: helps clear toxins and improve areas of cellulite; eases the chest and breathing in colds and influenza; eases anxiety, depression, and stress, helps to relieve insomnia and disturbed dreams.

Suggested blends: to detoxify, first use a skin brush on dry skin to boost the circulation, then add 4 drops grapefruit, 3 drops lemon, and 3 drops juniper to 4 teaspoons (20 ml) carrier oil for an evening massage of the affected areas. To relieve chest infections, add 3 drops grapefruit and 2 drops cedarwood to a bowl of nearly boiling water and inhale the vapor for 20 minutes; add the same drops to 2 teaspoons (10 ml) carrier oil afterward and massage the chest.

To ease insomnia and anxiety, add 2 drops grapefruit and 3 drops sandalwood to a warm bath and relax in the water; add the same drops to 2 teaspoons (10 ml) carrier oil and massage the skin afterward.

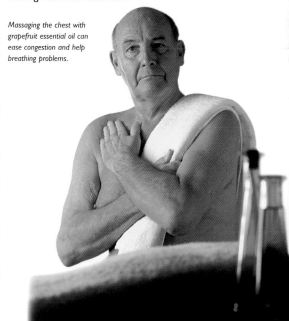

Massaging the chest with grapefruit essential oil can ease congestion and help breathing problems.

Bergamot

Citrus bergamia

Bergamot is a small and very bitter orange. It is grown in Italy, where it has been used in traditional remedies for many years.

Plant profile: bergamot is a small bitter orange grown in the Lombardy region of Italy near the town of Bergamo. The fruit has long been used in the traditional medicine of the area as a remedy for fevers and low immunity. The essential oil from the peel is best known as the flavoring of Earl Grey tea, giving the drink a fresh, citrusy flavor.

Safety information: bergamot is strongly phototoxic; avoid exposing the skin to strong sunlight or sunbeds for at least 12 hours after application. FCF (furano-coumarin free) bergamot oil is available with the phototoxic constituent removed, but the aroma of the oil is much reduced.

Fragrance profile: fresh, bright, citrusy, and sweet, developing softer, rounder, and warmer tones later.

Main uses: boosts immunity, helps to combat colds, influenza, and respiratory complaints; eases the symptoms of vaginal thrush; soothes anxiety, depression, helps to lift low spirits, and combat stress.

Suggested blends: to help boost the immune system, add 2 drops bergamot, 2 drops tea tree, and 1 drop black pepper to an evening bath and relax in the water; then add the same drops of essential oil to 2 teaspoons (10 ml) carrier oil and massage the chest area.

For thrush, add 2 drops bergamot and 3 drops sandalwood to a warm bath to soothe the area.

To ease stress and anxiety, vaporize 3 drops bergamot and 3 drops frankincense to create a warm and uplifting aroma.

Bergamot and tea tree oils help to improve general immunity.

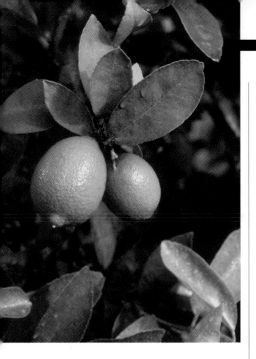

Safety information: lime is moderately phototoxic; you should avoid exposing the skin to strong sunlight or a sunbed for at least 12 hours after application.

Fragrance profile: bitter, green, and fresh with a powerful zest and sharp fruity notes.

Main uses: helps detoxify and improve areas of cellulite; eases chest infections, respiratory complaints, and catarrh; clears the head and improves concentration.

Suggested blends: to detoxify, use a skin brush to stimulate the circulation, then add 2 drops lime, 3 drops juniper, and 5 drops cypress to 4 teaspoons (20 ml) carrier oil and massage affected areas, as an evening treatment. To relieve respiratory complaints, add 3 drops lime and 3 drops eucalyptus to a large bowl of nearly boiling water and inhale the vapors, twice daily for 20 minutes. To clear the head, increase alertness, and improve the atmosphere in stuffy rooms, vaporize 3 drops lime and 3 drops peppermint.

Fresh green limes are popular in Caribbean cooking. They are also an excellent source of vitamin C.

Lime

Citrus aurantifolia

Plant profile: an evergreen citrus tree, this is thorny with smooth aromatic leaves and small white flowers which turn into the fruits. Limes are about half the size of lemons and are a rich green in color. Limes are an excellent source of vitamin C and are widely used in cookery recipes from the West Indies. The oil is expressed from the peel. The main centers of production are Florida, Cuba, and Central America.

Vaporize a mixture of peppermint and lime essential oils to help improve concentration.

Simple Essential Oil Skincare

Essential oils can be used as the basis of a simple and effective skincare routine. They are particularly effective when used at night, because lying horizontally promotes an excellent supply of blood to your face for maximum absorption of essential oils through the skin. Use the chart below to identify your skin type and choose the blends that will be most suitable for you.

Skin types

Normal—smooth and supple, clear in appearance, fine-textured
Dry—dull-textured, dehydrated, tends to tighten up in wind or warm temperatures
Mature—evident expression lines and slackness around eyes and mouth, less elasticity
Oily—shiny, with large obvious pores, tendency to blemishes
Combination—a greasy patch over forehead, nose, and chin; dry cheek areas
Sensitive—often very pale, sensitive to sunlight and cosmetics, allergic tendency

Jojoba carrier oil is one of the best natural skin cleansers and is suitable for all types.

Cleanse

One of the best all-round skin cleansers is jojoba oil, a liquid wax from the jojoba bean. This wax is very similar to the skin's own oils, and literally dissolves dirt out of the pores. Even greasy skin can benefit, and jojoba conditions all skin types well. A small amount of blend on an absorbent cotton pad goes a long way. Use the cleansing blend before you get in your bath, so the steam from the bath can further open the pores before you use your toner.

Add one of the following blends to 4 teaspoons (20 ml) jojoba oil:

Normal/dry/mature skin: 2 drops frankincense, 4 drops sandalwood, 4 drops orange.

Oily/combination skin: 2 drops juniper, 3 drops cypress, 5 drops lemon.

Sensitive skin (half the proportions): 2 drops roman chamomile, 3 drops lavender.

These blends should be used within 4 weeks. They can be kept at room temperature or for longer in the refrigerator.

Tone

Good drug stores and essential oil suppliers sell floral waters, the by-products of the distillation process, which make very good toners. Use a small amount on an absorbent cotton pad to freshen the skin before the moisturizing treatment. The following flower waters are recommended:

Normal/dry/mature skin: pure rose water or pure neroli water.

Floral waters make very gentle skin toners. Good drug stores will stock them.

Oily/combination skin: pure lavender water.

Sensitive skin: pure chamomile water or pure rose water.

Floral waters will last up to six months if kept in the refrigerator.

Moisturize

Nighttime facial treatment oils have a shelf life of about four weeks and can be made up either in sweet almond oil, recommended for dry or mature skins, or jojoba, for all skin types.

Add to 4 teaspoons (20 ml) of carrier oil:

Normal/dry/mature skin: 2 drops rose, 3 drops neroli, 5 drops frankincense.

Oily/combination skin: 3 drops geranium, 3 drops cypress, 4 drops lemon.

Sensitive skin (half proportions): 3 drops roman chamomile, 2 drops rose.

Massage a small amount into your face for 10 minutes, using upward strokes on your cheeks and tiny circles around your eye sockets and over your forehead. Be careful not to wipe the blend into your eyes.

Special Massage Blends

Here are some special massage blends for you to try, for physical, mood-related, and seasonal reasons. They are all designed to be made up in 4 teaspoons (20 ml) carrier oil, such as sweet almond, jojoba, or grapeseed, a lighter and less greasy base oil. They all have a four-week shelf life. Massage relevant areas gently, using relaxing sweeping movements. Sometimes you may wish to work on yourself, but it can be soothing to let someone else—a close friend or partner—massage you.

Physical Tonics

Here are four blends for hard-working areas of the body which are constantly under strain.

Super muscle tone: for sports massage to energize and strengthen the muscles—4 drops rosemary, 2 drops lemongrass, and 4 drops ginger.

Barefoot bliss: a massage blend to help cool and soothe tired and aching feet after a long day—3 drops peppermint, 3 drops black pepper, and 4 drops lavender.

Chest relief: a wonderful blend for a chest massage to ease respiratory problems—

Massage blends firmly into the limbs for the best effect.

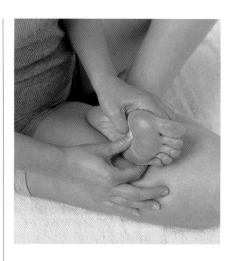

A foot massage warms and relaxes tired feet. It feels even better if someone else does it for you!

3 drops cedarwood, 3 drops frankincense, and 4 drops lemon.

Neck and shoulder rescue: ask a friend or your partner to massage this blend into your aching muscles—2 drops vetiver, 3 drops ginger, and 5 drops lavender.

Mood Mixtures

Here are some ideas for more subtle blends
with rich aromas. You will find them useful
for lifting the spirits and easing emotional
stresses and strains.

Beat the blues: 3 drops orange, 4 drops
grapefruit, and 3 drops sandalwood makes a
wonderful relaxing, uplifting, and de-stressing
blend for massage.

PMT reviver: at that low time in your
monthly cycle, try a blend of 4 drops
palmarosa, 2 drops patchouli, and 4 drops
bergamot for an evening massage blend.

On cloud nine: when you need to escape
and have no cares in the world, try 4 drops
grapefruit, 2 drops neroli, and 4 drops
cardamom for a dreamy aroma.

Tropical retreat: create an exotic mood
with 2 drops ylang ylang, 4 drops mandarin,
and 4 drops sandalwood—this is a fruity, rich,
and floral feast for the senses.

Seasonal Treats

As your energies vary, you may find that you
need different massage blends to pick you up
at different times of the year. Massage is
particularly effective after a bath, as the skin
absorbs the blend better. Spending time being
massaged also helps improve your sleep—
when you rest like this, your whole body can
restore itself and your mind can be at peace.

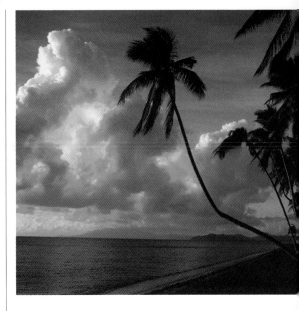

*Inhale the aromas of the oils in the blends and float off into your
own haven of tranquility—a tropical beach, for example.*

Springtime freshener: to help to revitalize
and energize you after the long drag of
wintertime—4 drops lemon, 3 drops juniper,
and 3 drops peppermint.

Summer skin food: use the following blend
in 4 teaspoons (20 ml) jojoba oil to nourish
the skin deeply—3 drops sandalwood, 2 drops
patchouli, and 5 drops frankincense.

Fall spiritual reviver: to uplift you
as the nights draw in—4 drops mandarin,
3 drops may chang, and 3 drops coriander.

Winter energizer: for aches, stiffness, and
low vitality—2 drops vetiver, 3 drops
lemongrass, and 5 drops nutmeg.

Essential Oils in Everyday Life

Essential oils are a wonderful and natural way to keep your environment fresh and to raise your energy levels. They are very portable and can easily be adapted to suit different locations and needs. Here are some ideas for using oils simply and effectively.

Home

In your home, essential oils help to personalize your living space.

Be careful to add the right number of drops of essential oil to your blends. This is important when blending for children.

Kitchen

This is one of the most frequently used and also most potentially accident-prone areas. Always keep lavender and tea tree to hand—you can use either oil neat for cuts, burns, scalds, and other mishaps (put 2 drops on an absorbent cotton pad). A kitchen spray to remove stale odors and freshen counters can be made in a pump-action spray bottle filled with a scant ½ cup/100 ml water, 10 drops peppermint, and 15 drops lemon. Shake the bottle and spray mist into the air, or spray counters and wipe them down.

A pump-action spray bottle helps to spread essential oils over a much wider area.

Dining room

A vaporizer adds atmosphere to a dinner party. For example, a festive gathering can be fragranced with 3 drops mandarin and 3 drops nutmeg, or a summer party with 3 drops may chang and 3 drops orange. One dose of essential oils in a vaporizer will last up to 2 hours.

Living room

Again, a vaporizer can clear the atmosphere, neutralize pet odors, and freshen the air. A combination like 3 drops tea tree and 3 drops lemon helps if someone has a cold or influenza. After a party the night before, 3 drops peppermint and 3 drops rosemary is very uplifting and refreshing.

Child's bedroom

An electric vaporizer is recommended for
safety reasons. Essential oils can really help
sleep. Add 3 drops lavender and 3 drops orange
for a soothing aroma; or 3 drops lavender and
3 drops eucalyptus if there are chest problems.
Try to start the vaporizer at least 10 minutes
before your child goes to bed—this spreads the
fragrance into the room as they fall asleep.

Travel

Essential oils can help you on the move.

Car

Vaporizers are available that plug into the
cigarette lighter socket, or you can put oils on
a tissue. On long journeys, 3 drops peppermint
and 3 drops rosemary will help you stay alert.

*Keep a tissue in your pocket when you're traveling on long
journeys—you can inhale oils from it when you have a break.*

*Vaporizing oils in a bedroom will improve the quality of sleep and
scent the room delightfully as well.*

Trains and airplanes

Carry one or two essential oils with you
and put a few drops onto a tissue to inhale.
Lavender will help you relax, peppermint and
rosemary will wake you up, and lemon or tea
tree will help ease sinus congestion.

Buying and Storing Essential Oils

Here are some simple guidelines to follow to help you get the best out of your essential oil collection.

Buying Oils

There are many essential oil suppliers now selling to the public, and there is, unfortunately, a huge variation in the quality and therapeutic effectiveness of the oils available. True essential oils are not just a manufactured product, they are produced year by year and harvests can be affected by many environmental changes. Cheap essential oils are much more likely to be synthetic copies than the genuine article. Check that your supplier sources oils directly from growers.

You need to buy your oils in dark glass bottles to protect them from UV light. Oils should also have a drop dispenser in the neck of the bottle to release one drop at a time to help you calculate your blends. This is also an important safety feature: open-necked bottles

Many plants are expensive to harvest and these oils can be costly to buy. However, their divine scent makes it all worthwhile!

are a risk to children, who may swallow the contents. In any case, keep all essential oils well out of children's reach.

Storing Oils

Essential oils degrade with time. Their constituents oxidize and become unstable, smelling rancid. The cooler and more tightly closed they are kept, the longer the shelf life. How long you keep your oils depends on the storage temperature: in a refrigerator, most oils last up to two years, citrus oils one year.

Dark glass bottles with integrated stoppers or drop dispensers are vital if you are planning to use a lot of essential oils.

Always keep essential oils cool and out of direct sunlight. They keep well in the refrigerator.

At room temperature, most oils last up to one year, citrus oils six months. The shelf life is calculated from the first day you open a new bottle. Write a date on the label or place a sticker on the bottle to remind you of the use-by date. If you are keeping oils in the refrigerator, you are advised to put them in an airtight box first to stop the fragrances spreading to milk and dairy products! Out of the refrigerator, keep the oils tightly closed, in the dark, and in a cool place. Do not use essential oils once they have gone past their shelf life, because they are then more likely to cause skin reactions.

Keeping essential oils in the refrigerator extends their shelf life. Make sure that the bottles are airtight at all times.

Recommended Suppliers

In the USA you are recommended to contact

National Association for Holistic Aromatherapy (NAHA) for details of suppliers: 2000 2nd Avenue, Suite 206, Seattle WA 98121
Tel: (206) 256-0741
www.naha.org

The following suppliers do mail order and sell high-quality ranges of essential oils.

Aromatherapy Products Ltd (suppliers of the Tisserand range, selling to 30 countries) Newtown Road, Hove, East Sussex BN3 7BA, UK
Tel: +44 (0)1273 325666;
Fax: +44 (0)1273 208444
Call them for your nearest stockist or mail order enquiries.

Essentially Oils Ltd
8–10 Mount Farm, Junction Road, Chipping Norton, Oxfordshire OX7 6NP, UK
Tel: +44 (0)1608 659544;
Fax: +44 (0)1608 659566
www.essentiallyoils.com
email: sales@essentiallyoils.com

Useful Addresses and Websites

USA & Canada

American Alliance of Aromatherapy
P.O. box 309
Depose Bay, OR 97341, USA
Phone (503) 392-4005

Association of Massage Theraphies and Wholistic Practitioners (AMTWP)
#207, 17878 - 106 Avenue
Edmonton, AB T5S 1V4, Canada
Phone: (780) 484-2010
email: admin@amtwp.org

Atlantic Institute of Aromatheraphy
16018 Saddlestring drive
Tampa, FL 33613, USA
Phone: (813) 265-2222
Email: sylia@AtlanticInstitute.com
www.AtlanticInstitute.com

California School of Herbal Studies
PO Box 39,
Forestville, CA 95436, USA
www.cshs.com

Herb Research Foundation
1007 Pearl Street, Suite 200,
Boulder, CO 80302, USA
www.herbs.org

International Aromatherapists & tutors Association (IATA)
268 Lakeshore Road East, Suite 226,
Oakville. ON L6J 7S4, Canada
Phone: (905) 822-9603
www.aroma-iata.com

National Association for Holistic Aromatheraphy (NAHA)
P.O. Box 17622
Boulder, CO 80308, USA
Phone: (415) 546-6785
www.naha.org

Australia

**Australian College of Natural
Medicine Inc.**
609-611 Camberwell Road,
Camberwell, Victoria 3124, Australia
Tel. +0061 0398 599 288
e-mail: acum@vicnet.net.au

**International Federation of
Aromatherapists**
PO Box 786, Templestowe,
Victoria 3106, Australia
Tel. +0061 1902 240 125
www.ifa.org.au

United Kingdom

**Aromatheraphy and Allied Practitioners'
Association (AAPA)**
8 George Street,
Croydon, surrey, CRO IPA, UK
Phone: +44 (0) 20 8680 7761
www.aromatheraphyuk.net
e-mail: aromatheraphyuk@aol.com

**International Federation of Professional
Aromatheraphy (IFPA)**
82 Ashby Road
Hinckley, Leicester, LE10 ISN, UK
Phone: +44 (0) 14 5563 7987
admin@ifaroma.org
http://ifaroma.org

crystals

Introduction

The world of crystals and jewels never ceases to fascinate us. Even in our everyday language we talk about a brilliant idea being "a gem," or about things being "as clear as crystal." Ask anyone what is the most valuable thing they can think of and many will answer "diamonds"—didn't Marilyn Monroe claim they were "a girl's best friend"?

An engagement ring containing a diamond or other gems is given as a symbol of something rare and precious that will last for ever. At the heart of our deep and long-lasting regard for these valuable and beautiful glittering gifts of the Earth is the idea that they are eternally special.

Engagement rings containing diamonds are a symbol of eternal and enduring love.

Fortunately, as well as precious stones, there are crystals like quartz, amethyst, moonstone, or garnet, which are also beautiful and much more affordable, either as jewelry, stones for a collection, or for healing purposes. This section will explore all of these aspects, especially the use of stones as tools for balancing the energies of body, mind, and spirit. This is a practice with deep historical roots; many stones have ancient associations with different physical or mental conditions. In India to this very day, gems are ground to a powder and mixed with water, then drunk for their healing properties, just as they were hundreds of years ago. In the Crystal Index, found later in this section on pages 147–179, we shall link 32 minerals and stones to their different colors and learn their geological

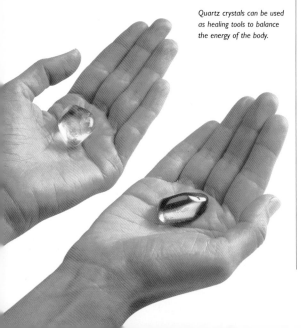

Quartz crystals can be used as healing tools to balance the energy of the body.

The brilliant luster of diamonds endeared them to Marilyn Monroe's character Lorelei Lee in Gentlemen Prefer Blondes.

the information given on particular stones will help you to realize why.

Bringing crystals into your personal space is a way of creating a connection with the Earth, since all crystals are born and grow within our planet's structure. If you use them with care and respect, crystals will share with you the positive energy of their light, color, and beauty. Whether you simply collect or wear them or use them to enhance your energy, crystals are a source of wonder. Enjoy this crystal journey through the worlds of geology, history, legend, and healing.

characteristics, as well as their history and healing uses.

Crystals can be used to beautify and clear the energies of your environment, as tools for meditation and contemplation, and of course can also be worn on your person. Perhaps the wearing of jewelry will take on a different meaning when you discover some of the fascinating geological and historical facts about the stones. You may find that you have already instinctively brought crystals into your environment and

The vibrant purple hues of an amethyst crystal have a soothing effect on the mind.

Mother Earth: Planet of Rebirth

Our story starts with the creation of the Earth—with the origin of minerals in the very structure of the planet on which we live. Minerals are natural, inorganic chemical substances. Approximately 2,500 different types exist.

The mineral kingdom provides the chemical building blocks for everything on the Earth: rocks, plants, animals—and humans. About 90 percent of each of us is made of water, and the rest is minerals!

The Earth is Always Moving

The Earth originally formed out of clouds of gas and the dust of other stars. Heavy elements like nickel and iron sank to form the hot core, which is still molten, made of liquid

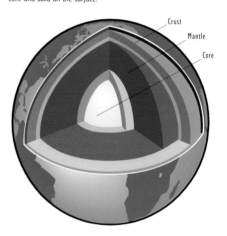

The Earth is made up of different layers. These are liquid at the core and solid on the surface.

Crust

Mantle

Core

minerals that are slowly pushed up to the surface. Lighter minerals such as silicon and oxygen, the ingredients of quartz, form part of a thicker, sometimes semi-molten layer called the mantle. Finally, the very lightest minerals float up to the surface of the Earth. This part, which is where we live and walk, is called the crust. Earthquake zones or volcanic areas like

Flowing red-hot lava spills onto the Earth's surface after a volcanic eruption.

The Three Main Types of Rocks

Igneous: these layers originally formed as a mass of molten rock (called magma) deep inside the Earth's core. They rise to cover the crust through cracks or volcanic eruptions. Combined with water in the upper layers just below the surface, magma may form quartz crystals in large gaps called veins. Depending on the other minerals present, gems like emeralds or aquamarine may form.

Metamorphic: these are rock layers that have been changed after their original formation, usually by increases in pressure, heat, water vapor, or chemical reactions. For example, layers of clay and sand sinking into the crust under pressure can form the mineral compound corundum, otherwise known as sapphire or ruby.

Sedimentary: these are layers of soft rock on the surface, formed by the actions of wind and water on surface minerals. The most common is limestone.

Crystals form in pockets or areas of space between rock layers. Mining techniques have developed to harvest these treasures.

Rubies are one of the most precious gems that can be found in the world.

Mount Etna in Sicily show how thin the crust actually is. As heat from the Earth's core pushes minerals upward, cooler rocks sink, then melt at the core and are pushed up to the surface again. The Earth is constantly shifting and recycling minerals.

The Earth's Floating Crust

The Earth's crust literally floats on the mantle. It is made up of different sections or "plates"; wherever these collide with each other, the pressure folds rocks into mountains or bursts open volcanoes. Deep in the oceans, cracks in the crust let new mineral masses grow, pushing continents sideways. This movement happens because of the cycles of rising heated minerals and sinking cooler layers. New sources of precious stones and gems continue to be found because the Earth's surface is never static, and the location of stones and gems is always changing. Even though this process takes millions of years, new mineral layers are continually being formed within the Earth's structure.

The Making of Crystals

The many compounds of minerals that are found in the Earth's crust have been classified into different groups. Here are some of the most significant categories, which include many of the stones that you are likely to encounter.

Crystal Shapes and Inclusions

A crystal is a chemical compound that has changed naturally from a liquid to a solid with a regular geometric form and smooth sides. Crystals follow geometrical principles as their molecules arrange themselves. Quartz crystals divide and subdivide themselves along a hexagonal axis, meaning they typically have six sides called "faces." The points are called "terminations" and crystals with points at both ends are "double terminated." It is also possible for twin crystals to form like mirror images of each other. Some crystals contain specks that look like flaws, but which are simply air bubbles or specks of other minerals; these are called "inclusions." Rutilated quartz contains many hairlike strands of rutile, a mineral sometimes called "Venus' hair."

Clear quartz crystals make good healing wands because of their shape.

Crystals are mined from deep inside the Earth's crust. This is not a modern phenomenon—mining has been carried out for centuries.

Crystal Extraction Methods

In ancient times, our ancestors gathered crystals from the surface of the Earth quite spontaneously, and even today mineral enthusiasts still do this. Mining for metals and crystals has been happening since the Stone Age, with very well established workings in the Middle East during Roman times. Modern industrial mining for many kinds of precious stones takes place extensively in countries such as Sri Lanka, Brazil, and South Africa. When you buy a crystal, it is worth remembering it has come via the miner, the wholesaler, the retailer, and others before reaching you. This is why cleansing the crystals you buy is so important (see pages 146–147).

Amber is fossilized tree resin and is millions of years old.

Pearls are another example of an organic material. In this case, the origin is animal.

Organic Minerals

"Organic" in this context means something with plant or animal origins. A few such minerals exist. Amber, for example, is the fossilized resin of an ancient pine tree. Pearls form when a grain of sand irritates the inner lining of the pearl oyster.

Main Groups of Metals and Crystals

Native elements *(uncombined with other elements)* gold, silver, platinum, copper, carbon (as diamond).

Sulphides *(metal plus sulphur)* iron plus sulphur makes pyrite (fool's gold).

Oxides *(main group is silicon dioxide, making quartz)* clear quartz, amethyst, rose quartz, smoky quartz; also microcrystalline forms called chalcedony, the name given to crystals such as carnelian and tiger's eye because of their waxy or translucent appearance. Opals are similar to quartz but are made of silicon dioxide and water. Aluminum oxide forms the compound corundum, whose red and blue forms are rubies and sapphires respectively.

Silicates within this group are feldspars comprising a huge number of crystals, very common in the Earth's crust. Moonstone and labradorite are varieties of feldspar made up of sodium and calcium. Another large silicate group are garnets, which may be rich in aluminum, iron, or chromium depending on their location. Other silicate minerals are tourmaline and the beryls, including aquamarine and emerald.

Royal Crystals

Crystals and precious stones have long been valued as hunting tools, carvings, jewelry, or icons. They were used as badges of royalty and power, symbolizing the unique status of kings and queens. They are so precious that wars have been fought over them.

The Ancient Egyptians were mining emeralds, peridot, lapis lazuli, and other precious stones over 3,000 years ago. They were highly skilled in polishing and setting in gold and their work can still be admired in their relics, especially the treasures of the Pharaohs. For thousands of years, diamonds and other gems have been mined in India, Sri Lanka, and Burma (now called Myanmar), as well as countries in South America and Africa. The ancient Mayan and Chinese civilizations produced exquisite carvings of jade and emerald.

Queen Elizabeth II wearing the Imperial State Crown, one of the most important items of regalia in the Crown Jewels.

The Tower of London, surrounded by the famous ravens, is where the British Crown Jewels can be seen.

The British Royal Family's Crown Jewels

The Jewel House in the Tower of London contains all of the British Royal Family's regalia. The most famous element of this collection is St. Edward's Crown, which is worn by the reigning monarch. The first Crown Jewels were assembled by King Edward the Confessor in the eleventh century. In

The Koh-i-noor, one of the largest diamonds in the world, is set in the crown of Queen Elizabeth the Queen Mother.

The History of the Koh-i-noor

The Koh-i-noor is one of the largest single diamonds in the world and was first owned by the Rajah of Malwa in India in 1304. It has a weight of 186 carats. To put this weight into perspective, most modern diamond engagement rings weigh approximately 0.25 to 1 carat. For several hundred years, the jewel belonged to various Indian emperors. In 1739, the Shah of Persia invaded Delhi and pillaged the city to find the legendary diamond. He was told that the defeated emperor had the jewel hidden in his turban. He invited his captive to exchange turbans. Unrolling the cloth, the Shah found the jewel. He cried out "Koh-i-noor!," or "Mountain of light!"—which remained its name.

When Lahore, the capital of Punjab, was annexed to British India in 1849, the stone passed to the East India Company, who presented it to Queen Victoria in 1850. It was displayed at the Crystal Palace exhibition, disappointing viewers because it did not appear to sparkle enough. Queen Victoria therefore had the diamond re-cut, reducing it from 186 carats to 108.93.

In 1911 the stone was set in the crown of Queen Mary. In 1937 the diamond was reset, this time in the crown of Queen Elizabeth the Queen Mother.

1216, King John Plantagenet subsequently lost them in quicksand in East Anglia. The next collection also had a rather checkered history. During the Civil War in 1649, Oliver Cromwell ordered them to be broken up; however, remnants were saved and later incorporated into the new regalia fashioned for King Charles II when he ascended the throne in 1661. Today, the collection is priceless. In the early twentieth century, the largest diamond ever found, the Cullinan, was cut into four segments. One segment, known as the "Star of Africa," is carried in the Sovereign's Scepter. It weighs more than 530 carats and has 74 facets, making it the world's largest cut diamond.

Crystals Today

In the early twentieth century, fabulous jewels began to adorn famous Hollywood movie stars and be seen regularly on the screen and in magazines. It is not surprising that these legendary bejeweled icons have become as admired as royalty.

Famous Women and their Gems

The screen goddess Marlene Dietrich loved emeralds, especially those carved into smooth-domed cabochons. She once lost a 37-carat emerald ring in a cake mixture and found it again in a piece of the cake! Elizabeth Taylor has been one of Hollywood's greatest stars, with an amazing jewelry collection. The Taylor–Burton diamond given to her by Richard Burton weighs almost 70 carats. She also has a collection of dazzling emerald jewelry that once belonged to a Russian Grand Duchess. Jacqueline Kennedy Onassis also collected dazzling pieces, especially from her second husband Aristotle Onassis. His engagement ring to her was auctioned at Sotheby's for $2.6 million in 1996. When Princess Diana's fine sparkling sapphire and diamond engagement ring was originally shown to the world's press, it sparked a fashion for copies of the design.

Marlene Dietrich, the legendary screen icon, adored emeralds, especially when they were cut into smooth, rounded cabochons.

In the film Diamonds are Forever, *James Bond discovers the power of diamonds and what others will do to get them.*

Crystal Movies

Even in our sophisticated age, nothing beats a good adventure story, as film-makers know very well. The idea of a dangerous hunt for a huge, priceless emerald inspired the film *Romancing the Stone*, and the James Bond epic *Diamonds are Forever*, as well known for the song as for the story, deals with diamonds as a source of staggering wealth and power. In the 1970s and early 1980s, the "Superman" movies introduced new ideas: namely that crystals could hold energy and even power spacecraft! It also explored the idea that diamonds could hold information—an idea realized in the development of the silicon chip. This interesting shift in presentation coincided with a general interest in crystals for healing.

The New Age— Expanding Crystal Awareness

Since the 1960s, crystals have been used increasingly as healing tools. Many writers have linked this awareness to the New Age, a rise in spiritual consciousness, particularly toward the dawn of the New Millennium. In fact, crystals have been used for healing since before Egyptian times. However, with advances in geology and quantum physics, the structure and energy of crystals is beginning to be understood in different terms. People are made up of the same elements as crystals. We are made of the same minerals that are recycled by the Earth in spite of the fact that we are organic beings, and minerals are inorganic. Perhaps one way of explaining the response to crystal energies is to say we subtly recognize elements that are in us all.

A rose quartz crystal placed on the body can enhance relaxation and feelings of well-being and happiness.

Crystals, Colors, and Chakras

One of the most striking things about crystals is their color. This is often what first attracts us, such as when our eye is drawn to the vivid green of emeralds or the deep purple of amethysts. Different colors can affect us physically and emotionally—for example, the blue-green of the sea is calming to the eyes and the spirit.

The color spectrum can be used as a model for understanding the different energies at work in our bodies.

Color Healing

If you take a cut-glass pendulum and hang it in a sunny window, your walls will be covered in many dancing rainbows showing the seven pure color shades of the spectrum— red, orange, yellow, green, blue, indigo, and violet. The white light that splits into all these colors is the only part of the spectrum we can see, although insects and some animals can see infrared and ultraviolet waves too.

In ancient Egyptian times, healers chose ingredients for their patients on the basis of the color of the problem. For example, red was for blood, purple for bruising, yellow for jaundice. The wearing of

When we see blue or green shades, in nature or elsewhere, these act as a relaxant and have a calming effect on us.

The rainbow colors to be found in crystals show all the colors of the spectrum. Specific colors are used in different healing methods.

clothes or jewelry of that color came to be associated with the prevention of the condition; if you had poor circulation, you were advised to wear red. (This is because cold feet do become warmer more quickly in red socks than in any other color.)

By the twentieth century, scientists were beginning to experiment with light waves, noting that the properties of the red and orange rays were "warmer," and the blue and purple rays "cooler," with the color green in the middle as a balance. These days, light frequencies directed through lasers are being used in surgery and for healing wounded tissue.

The Chakra System

Several thousand years ago, in India, the energy frequencies of the body were perceived as being on seven different levels, each corresponding to an area in the body, centered in a "chakra," or "wheel." The white light of universal energy was considered to enter through the crown of the head and then modulated in frequency through each of the color levels from violet at the crown to red at the base of the spine. This ancient model is widely used in healing work and yoga practice today.

Meditating on the colors of the rainbow can bring about strong feelings of relaxation and calm.

Chakra	Color	Gland	Body Area
crown	violet	pineal	top of head
third eye	indigo	pituitary	mid-forehead
throat	blue	thyroid	throat
heart	green	thymus	center of chest
solar plexus	yellow	spleen	under diaphragm
sacrum	orange	ovaries/testes	lower abdomen
root	red	adrenals	base of spine

Within each color, shades are possible. Green can vary from yellow-green to emerald to dark green, but all shades relate to the heart chakra.

Small crystals can easily be placed on your body and around your living and working environment.

The way universal energy passes into the body is through the breath. As you breathe in—not just air but life force—the energy levels are maintained at appropriate levels. However, if there is disharmony, then other help may be needed. Colors and crystals can be used to rebalance diminished chakra energies.

Color Healing Chart

This color healing chart is designed to suggest links between colors, body energies, color effects, chakra centers, and crystals. The original seven colors of the spectrum have been expanded to include shades, as well as rays like silver. This chart corresponds exactly with the Crystal Index (pages 147–179), where individual stones are discussed in detail. Guided by the way you feel, you will be able to choose the appropriate colors to help you, as well as select useful crystals. You will find some simple crystal healing methods described on pages 180–181.

Some of these correspondences may be surprising. Black, for example, often has an undeserved negative association, but it can have quite a different meaning. In many healing traditions such as that of the Native Americans, for example, black is simply seen as the complement to white. Observing the night sky, the darkness creates the shadow that lets the light of the stars appear like diamonds on black velvet. Native American teachings revere the darkness as the source of mystery, the place from which all new things are born. Every creation myth on Earth relates the origin of the planet to a time of dark formlessness, out of which came light.

Here are some examples showing how you can use the chart. If you feel cold and lacking in energy, you will see that red is a warming color and garnets are suggested. You can either find some red in your wardrobe, or try wearing the crystal or meditating on it (see pages 184–185). If you are afraid of change, try wearing or meditating with labradorite. If you want to expand a relationship, wear amber colors or the stone. You will discover your own favorite colors and stones very quickly. If you find yourself using a lot of one particular stone or color, then that chakra clearly needs energizing.

Tumblestones are examples of small polished crystals that are very easy to carry around with you.

The Color Healing Chart

Color	Energy	Effect	Chakra	Stone	
Red	action	warming	root	garnet	
Orange	relationship	expanding	sacrum	amber	
Yellow	mental alertness	clearing	solar plexus	topaz	
Light Green	spontaneity	refreshing	heart	peridot	
Rich Green	love	harmonizing	heart	emerald	
Turquoise*	protection	strengthening	heart/thymus	turquoise	
Pale Blue	communication	soothing	throat	celestite	
Dark Blue	intuition	connecting	third eye	lapis lazuli	
Violet	insight	inspiring	crown	amethyst	
Pink	unconditional love	releasing	heart	rose quartz	
White	universal energy	healing	all chakras	clear quartz	
Black	universal mystery	visioning	root	obsidian	
Brown	rootedness	grounding	root	smoky quartz	
Iridescent	change	flowing	third eye	labradorite	
Gold	self-worth	revitalizing	crown	gold	
Silver	inner knowledge	calming	third eye	silver	

* Turquoise (blue-green) is often seen as corresponding to a minor chakra point, at the thymus gland in the upper chest, which supports the immune system.

Choosing and Caring for Crystals

Selecting the crystals you want and taking care of them is an important part of building a collection. This can become a very rewarding pastime as well as having interesting subtle effects on you and your living space.

Choosing Crystals

You will be attracted to stones because of their color, their shape or size, or even for more subtle reasons. Remember, we have discussed that you and crystals share mineral elements in common. Crystals have their own "frequency" thanks to the arrangement of their

To clean crystals and get rid of any negative energy that might be lingering, hold them under clear running water.

molecules—and so do you. This means that if a crystal jumps out at you or you feel sensations of tingling when you pick up a particular stone, then this is the one for you. It has been demonstrated with willing subjects that human electromagnetic energies change when crystals are brought near the body; you are simply reacting to the stone. You should trust that feeling and go with it (and just hope that you are not drawn to the most expensive ones!). Remember there is a difference between a naturally terminated crystal point such as quartz and a stone that has been polished, cut, or shaped. One is in a natural state and the other has been worked by human hands. They are equally beautiful, but they have different energies.

Cleansing Crystals

Having purchased your crystals, it makes sense to clean them. They have been mined, extracted, possibly tumbled or cut, sold to a wholesaler, transported, brought to sale, and

If you sit quietly and hold your crystal in your hands, you can "program" it with positive energy.

"Programing" Crystals

Programing a crystal means letting new energy flow into the crystal from you, making it uniquely yours. You could choose to charge it with the pink ray of unconditional love or visualize pure white universal light flowing down your arms, into your hands and filling the crystal. You can then ask the stone to continue to reflect that love in your personal space, and place it carefully wherever you think it needs to sit.

The Crystal Index

handled by many people before you. Cleansing is not just about removing dirt, grease, and dust, it also clears previous energies from the stone. Simply hold your crystal under flowing cold water for several minutes and visualize all other energy traces being dissolved. If you are not sure if the crystal is fully clear, ask in your mind and intuit the response, and repeat until you feel the stone is clear. Crystals should be cleaned regularly, especially if they are used for healing.

The Crystal Index covers the next 32 pages. You will find the stones arranged by color, corresponding to the chart on page 145. The color ray is explained in more detail, and then each stone is given a profile showing geological, geographical, historical, and healing information. As well as reading them all, try flipping the pages and stopping at a color that attracts you on a particular day. You may need that energy!

Amethyst reflects the color violet and brings inspiration into our hearts and minds. It is a very popular crystal for healing work.

Red

Red is the bright stimulating color of action. Wearing red is very energizing, and red gemstones help you feel dynamic and confident.

Ruby

Geology: Ruby is a variety of corundum, the second hardest known mineral, colored red by the element chromium. The most precious rubies can be rarer and more valuable than diamonds. Fine rubies glow like red-hot coals. Pinkish or darker red examples also occur. Some very rare stones show a six-pointed star effect in bright light due to bands of rutile in their structure. These are called star rubies.

Exquisitely carved rubies have been used as personal signet rings to seal documents for centuries.

Sources: In Myanmar, some ruby mines date from the Stone and Bronze Ages. Today this country is still the most famous source of rubies. Thailand produces rubies of a darker color and is the most important ruby trading center in the world.

History: "Ruby" comes from the Latin word *ruber* meaning red. Similar words are found in Persian and Sanskrit for both the stone and the color red. Rubies have been venerated for thousands of years. In the Old Testament, God places this "lord of gems" on Aaron's neck. The Bible also states that wisdom is "more precious than rubies."

Healing uses: Ruby lights a fire of courage within you, encouraging you to step beyond yourself to new possibilities. It increases your physical vitality and your physical energy, boosting your circulation and bringing strength to you. It is a stone that symbolizes power, leadership, and integrity.

Garnet

Geology: Garnets form in igneous and metamorphic rocks under high pressure, and occur in very precise symmetrical crystals with twelve diamond-shaped facets. They are mostly known for their deep red color, but can be found in pink, orange, and even green shades. Pyrope garnets have a dark ruby-red color, and rhodolite garnets are also popular, with a pinkish to purplish-red sheen.

The rich red hues of garnets mean that the stones make very attractive jewelry.

Sources: Pyrope garnets are mined in South Africa and also the USA, specifically in Utah and Arizona, where the common name for them is "anthill garnets." This is because tiny examples are excavated by ants when building their nests. The rhodolite variety are obtained from Africa, India, and Sri Lanka.

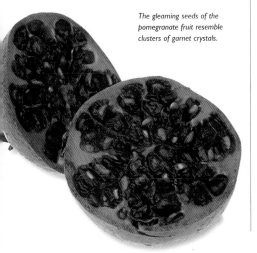

The gleaming seeds of the pomegranate fruit resemble clusters of garnet crystals.

History: The name "garnet" derives from the pomegranate, a fruit with dark seeds in bright red flesh resembling garnet clusters! Legend has it that Noah's Ark was lit up at night by a garnet lantern, and garnets have traditionally been used as a protective talisman when traveling.

Healing uses: Garnet provides a calm, grounding strength to the physical body. It helps you feel centered with a reservoir of inner strength and confidence. It is used to strengthen and regenerate the body, boosting the circulation and the reproductive energies.

Garnets can be quite large stones and look particularly beautiful when they are set in simple silver or gold.

Warning

Wearing red stones is not recommended for people with high blood pressure or heart problems.

Orange

Warm sunny shades of orange are very positive colors. Orange removes fear and replaces it with optimism, improving your relationships with others.

Amber

Geology: Amber is fossilized resin or tree sap from the ancient pine tree *Pinus succinifera* and has taken approximately 25–50 million years to harden. Amber is also called succinite. Thousands of samples have been found containing whole insects, pollen grains, and ancient plants. Amber is organic because of its plant origin. It is usually found in yellow, gold, or orange shades, but red, brown, and green varieties also exist.

Amber has been worn as an ornament for thousands of years.

Sources: Fine amber is mainly found in the Baltic states and the Dominican Republic.

History: Archeological finds reveal that humankind has used and revered amber since the Stone Age. In ancient Greece, amber was considered to be the juice or essence of the setting sun. In the epic poem the *Odyssey*, Homer mentions amber being given as a princely gift. In Roman times, amber artifacts were regarded as being more valuable than slaves.

Healing uses: Amber helps lift your spirits. It builds your physical vitality and positively charges your energy levels. It shields you from negativity from other people or from your environment. It is used to clear and rebalance the heart, the abdomen, and lower back areas.

Some examples of amber contain whole insects preserved within them. These make interesting pieces of jewelry.

Carnelian

Geology: Carnelian is a variety of chalcedony, a kind of quartz made up of tiny finely grained microcrystals. It is found in shades of apricot, deep orange, and even red-brown, and good quality stones have a translucent sheen. It is easily carved and has often been used for seals or signet rings.

Carnelian stones have a deep warm color. They also have an attractive mellow sheen.

Sources: Carnelian comes from Brazil, Uruguay, and also from India. Indian carnelian grows redder on exposure to the sun. It is readily available in the form of small polished tumblestones.

History: As far back as 3000 BCE, carnelian and other gemstones were used in Mesopotamia and Egypt as amulets for protection. Carnelian was also reputed to be used as one of the twelve sacred stones set in the breastplate of Aaron. In the Middle Ages, powdered carnelian mixed with water was taken as a remedy against the plague. In medieval times, gemstones were often identified with different emotional states, and carnelian was seen as a healer of anger.

Healing uses: Carnelian helps to ease depression and gives you a sense of inner stability. It can also help to balance the mind when you are trying to tackle difficult mental tasks. Carnelian warms and stimulates the appetite and balances the female reproductive system, easing menstrual pain. It promotes a sense of attunement with oneself. Its energy is warm, joyful, and opening, particularly when it is placed on the lower abdominal area.

Carnelian was a popular healing gem in medieval times. It was used as a remedy against the plague.

Yellow

Yellow is a bright color that is stimulating to the mind; a positive radiance full of energy and zest. Yellow gemstones sparkle against the skin like sunlight.

Citrine

Golden yellow citrine is a beautiful stone to place in your environment.

Geology: Natural citrine is a pale yellow quartz with a gentle sparkle and sheen. True citrine tends to be light in color. Darker yellow or orange examples are very likely to be artificially heat-treated amethyst or smoky quartz. Such stones can often be detected by their reddish sheen. It is possible to obtain very large pieces of citrine as well as delicate crystal clusters and the six-sided terminations that are typical of quartz crystals in general.

Sources: Today most citrine is mined in Brazil in the state of Rio Grande do Sul. Some deposits also exist in Madagascar.

History: The name citrine derives from the French word *citron* (lemon), alluding to the pale yellow color. In the past, the stone was thought to protect against the venom of poisonous snakes.

Healing uses: Citrine clears your mind of conflicting thoughts and provides space to think. It is used to detoxify the body and has a beneficial effect on the kidneys, liver, and gall bladder. It tones the digestion and the circulation. It attracts abundance into your life, whether in the form of money or relationships. Try placing it beside your bed to help you sleep.

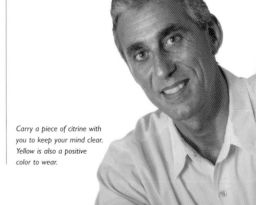

Carry a piece of citrine with you to keep your mind clear. Yellow is also a positive color to wear.

The ancient Egyptians associated yellow topaz with Ra, the sun god. In this wall painting, Ra is the figure sitting in the boat flanked by two baboons.

Topaz has a very effective cleansing effect on the body when it is used in healing.

Topaz

Geology: Topaz is a yellow gemstone that has been used for jewelry for centuries. It is mostly yellow in color, but it can also be found in orange, red, blue, and even green shades. It can form massive clusters of up to 220 pounds (100 kilograms) in weight and is one of the hardest minerals in nature. Its color has often caused it to be confused with the less valuable citrine, yet it has a beautiful transparent luster all of its own.

Sources: Brazil is known for high-quality yellow topaz, with other deposits occurring in Sri Lanka, Myanmar, and the USA. Russian topaz is pale blue in color.

History: Ancient Egyptians associated the yellow gemstone with Ra, the sun god, and the Romans with Jupiter, the king of the gods. It was used in protective amulets. A gem thought to have many mystical properties, topaz was said to change color in the presence of poisons in food or drink—it was even used to detect these. A stunning giant topaz is set in the Portuguese royal crown.

Healing uses: Yellow topaz is useful for focusing your mind on complex problems and generating fresh new ideas. Topaz is valued in healing as a detoxifying stone. It has particularly beneficial effects on the liver, gall bladder, and the whole body in general. Topaz also has a toning effect on the nervous system. It helps to enhance overall energy levels and brings inspiration and creativity.

Light Green

Light green is a gentle shade like new golden-green leaves in springtime. It is a youthful energy, fresh and subtle.

Peridot

Geology: Peridot is a variety of olivine, with a lovely pale-green color provided by iron, nickel, and chromium. It is a volcanic gem. In Hawaii on the island of Oahu, you can find volcanic olivine grains on the beaches. Peridot has also been found in meteorite deposits.

Sources: More than 3,500 years ago, the Egyptians used peridot from a mine on an island called Zeberget in the Red Sea. This continued to yield gems until after World War I. Today, most peridot is mined in Arizona, with specimens also found in Myanmar, Brazil, and Hawaii. In the 1990s a new deposit was discovered in the Pakistan-owned region of Kashmir.

Peridot stones have a gentle fresh green color, which is very lightening to the mind and spirit. It is used in healing to reduce stress and tension.

Peridot is said to have been a favorite stone of Queen Cleopatra, who must have appreciated its pale green color.

History: Legend has it that peridot was a favorite gemstone of Queen Cleopatra. Peridot is found decorating many medieval churches, including the Shrine of the Three Kings in Cologne Cathedral in Germany. Set in gold, the stone was traditionally credited with the power to drive away evil spirits. Some stones were large enough to be carved into drinking goblets.

Healing uses: Peridot has a light, revitalizing effect on your mind and reawakens your appreciation of beauty. It is used in healing to revitalize the heart, spleen, and adrenal glands, toning the body and mind, reducing stress and tension. It activates a sense of joy within you.

Jade

Geology: Jade is the name applied to two ornamental stones from China and Central America, nephrite and jadeite. These are very similar in structure and used in similar ways. Jade is a beautiful stone mostly found in various shades of pale to vivid green. Jade is usually cut into smooth dome shapes called cabochons, as well as carved into bangles, beads, and statues. Dealers have to gamble when buying jade. They purchase a boulder with only a tiny opening visible from the outside. On splitting, the interior may be found to reveal fine stone or be worthless.

Jade occurs in soft and beautiful shades of green. It looks particularly lovely when carved into statues.

became popular in Europe in the sixteenth century when beautiful artifacts began to be brought over from Central America.

Healing uses: Jade helps to balance emotional states, particularly in highly sensitive individuals. It can calm the heart and soothe away anxiety. Jade is often used in healing to bring the energy of unconditional love and peace into the heart, as well as nurturing and caring for the spirit.

Sources: Top quality jade (jadeite) now comes mostly from Myanmar and Guatemala. The main deposits of nephrite are found in Canada, Australia, the USA, and Taiwan.

History: Jade has been the royal gemstone of China for more than 4,000 years. Priceless jade artifacts were placed in the tombs of emperors as a symbol of their power and wealth. In Central America, jade was sacred to the Olmec, Mayan, and Toltec peoples, who carved it into masks and sacred relics. Jade

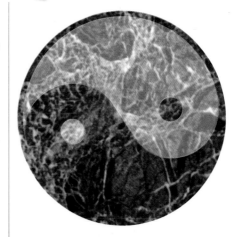

The energy of jade is balancing and harmonizing, as suggested by this yin and yang symbol.

Rich Green

Vivid shades of green are soothing to the eye, restful, and calming. Green blends yellow and blue, balancing warm and cool energies. Green stones are very beneficial to the heart chakra.

Emerald

Geology: Emerald is the green variety of beryl. Its color is caused by chromium

Darker green shades are very calming—they are particularly useful when working with the heart chakra.

and iron. True emeralds contain tiny inclusions and other flaws. Because emeralds grow in metamorphic layers of rock under pressure, the size of the gems is usually small, with larger examples being very rare.

Sources: Colombia, the producer of the astonishing emeralds associated with the Aztec empire, is still the main producer of fine stones today. Zambia and Brazil also produce top-quality emeralds, as do Zimbabwe, Pakistan, and Madagascar.

History: The Aztecs yielded up treasure to the conqueror Hernán Cortes, notably emeralds carved into fish and flowers, with some examples the size of a fist. The color of the stone made it particularly sacred to the ancient peoples of South America. Emeralds

were also found in ancient Egypt—Cleopatra had her own mines near the Red Sea.

Healing uses: The energy of emerald can help to connect you with your creative source. The green color links you to Nature. In healing, emerald is used to balance the heart and open it up to divine love.

True emeralds have a dramatic effect when set in jewelry. Here they are partnered with gold in a pair of stunning earrings.

Moldavite

Geology: Moldavite is a dark-green form of tektite, which is a kind of fused glass formed when meteor showers hit the Earth millions of years ago. Moldavite is not crystalline in structure; it has swirls, bobbles, and craters and forms unusual shapes due to its molten origin. Black and brown tektites exist, but rare dark-green moldavite is the most collectable.

Sources: Moldavia in Eastern Europe is considered to be the best source of green tektite. Fine examples are also found in Moldau in former Czechoslovakia, Thailand and Southeast Asia, Australia, and the USA.

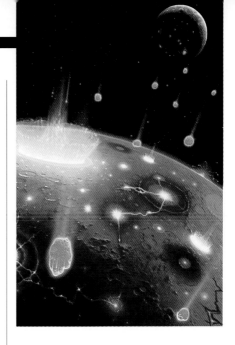

Moldavite falls to Earth from space in meteor showers. Meteorites containing moldavite fuse with geological deposits on the Earth.

Moldavite specimens exist in a range of unusual shapes and sizes.

History: Moldavite is fascinating because of its extraterrestrial origin. It is a fusion of elements from space with geological deposits on the surface of the Earth. It has sometimes been used for making jewelry.

Healing uses: Moldavite can be used to help connect you to deeper levels of spiritual awareness, from the earthly to other dimensions and realms of being. The stone reminds us that we are all travelers through space—even as we go about our daily lives. Our planet is sailing on a continual journey. In healing, the stone can be placed on the forehead to enhance spiritual awareness of our place in the cosmos.

Turquoise

This shade is a fusion of green and blue, a cool and soothing balm to the heart and the emotions. Turquoise stones show up particularly well against darker skins.

Turquoise

Geology: Turquoise is a valuable mineral known scientifically as hydrated copper aluminium phosphate. Its color ranges from sky blue to various shades of blue-green; the more iron is present, the greener the shade. True specimens contain tiny crystalline deposits that can be seen only with a microscope. There are many fake turquoises on the market that have been stained or dyed. True turquoise is very porous and should not be cleaned with chemicals, just warm soapy water.

Sources: Iran produces very pale sky-blue turquoise with no green tinges and veins; Arizona and New Mexico also yield fine examples. Afghanistan and the Middle East are other sources of the mineral.

Fine turquoise jewelry is still made by talented Navajo craftspeople. The stone looks stunning when set in silver.

History: For thousands of years, Persia was the main source of turquoise. At Sinai in Egypt turquoise was being mined over 5,000 years ago. In Mexico, turquoise was revered as a stone fit only for the gods. In the southwest USA, the Native American Navajo continue to make fine turquoise jewelry set in silver.

Healing uses: Turquoise ignites courage in your heart and strengthens your awareness of all life forms. It is used in healing to tone the whole body, as well as easing the lungs, chest, and throat and boosting the immune system.

Turquoise is a protective stone that benefits and tones the whole of the immune system.

Aquamarine

Geology: Aquamarine is another variety of beryl, with a pale blue-green color like sea water—the meaning of its name.

Aquamarine is a popular stone and is most commonly set in silver. This shows off its delicate color to perfection.

The purer the blue shade, the more expensive the stone. Aquamarine forms hexagonal crystals and is found in coarse granite rocks. Some aquamarines are heat-treated to increase the blue color. The rough stones have a similar appearance to tourmaline.

Sources: Brazil is the leading producer of aquamarine, with the USA, Zambia, Mozambique, and Pakistan also yielding wonderful specimens.

History: Perhaps not surprisingly, there is a great deal of sea folklore and legends associated with aquamarine. It was said to be treasured by mermaids, and was carried by sailors to ensure their safety while at sea. The stone was also seen as a traditional guardian of marriage and it remains an appropriate token to give as an anniversary gift.

Healing uses: Aquamarine expands and uplifts your spirits and helps you think clearly. It is seen as enhancing self-expression and self-worth, particularly in the sphere of your chosen line of work. It has a gently purifying effect on the mind and body, particularly helping the energies of the thyroid, spleen, liver, and kidneys. In healing, aquamarine can be placed on the throat to balance the emotions and aid their clear verbal expression. Meditation with aquamarine can help to instil peace and calm in you.

Aquamarine is used to ease the throat in healing work. This aids clear verbal expression and enables the patient to communicate.

Pale Blue

Pale blue is very gentle and soothing to the nerves, the sight, and the emotions. Pale-blue stones emit a soft healing energy, which is very much needed in our mad, overexcited world.

Celestite

Geology: Celestite is a form of strontium sulphate. It is a clear transparent mineral with a very pale blue color deepening to blue-gray, a shade that is unique in the mineral kingdom. It forms larger clusters with pronounced bladed crystals, as well as smaller nodules with tiny inward-growing crystals.

The soft gray-blue of celestite can be used in your environment to soothe and calm the emotions.

Sources: The most abundant sources of celestite tend to be found in sedimentary rocks in the USA, particularly in New York, Michigan, and Ohio. Specimens also occur in Germany, Madagascar, and Sicily.

Celestite is also known as the stone of heaven, symbolizing the sacred energy of angels and celestial beings.

History: Celestite is highly valued among mineral collectors, and over the past few years has become more prominent in New Age shops because of its healing uses.

Healing uses: Celestite is the blue of a summer sky. It brings about expansion, open-heartedness, and room to breathe. Placed in a room, celestite calms the energy and is a wonderful focus for meditation. Some healers see it as a stone that symbolizes sacred personal space. In healing, it is used to enhance thyroid balance and reduce stress. If placed on the throat, it aids self-expression. It is also helpful for healers to use on themselves to replenish their energies.

Blue Moonstone

The changing light of the moon is reflected in the soft luster of moonstone.

Geology: Moonstone is a member of the feldspar family of minerals. It is a colorless or pale milky stone and when turned in the light, it shows a shimmering translucent blue sheen. This can be a silvery milky white in some specimens, but the blue stones are seen as more valuable. The stone contains layers that reflect light back at each other, creating the shimmering colored effect. The most effective way of enhancing this property is to cut and polish the stones into cabochons, so they are smooth, rounded domes.

Sources: Some of the best examples of moonstone are to be found in Madagascar, Sri Lanka, Australia, Brazil, and the USA.

Blue moonstone has a special gentle sheen. No wonder it is considered a sacred stone!

History: In India, moonstone is considered sacred and is dedicated to the goddess in her lunar forms.

Healing uses: Moonstone is associated with feminine energy and the cyclical nature of feminine rhythms. It brings balance and harmony to your emotions. It is a wonderful stone to mark changing feminine cycles through girlhood to puberty, motherhood, and wise-womanhood. It is seen as hormone-balancing and brings equilibrium to the senses. Worn as jewelry set in silver, it is one of the most attractive of the semi-precious stones.

Dark Blue

Rich dark-blue shades are cool and contemplative, bringing a meditative state of calm to the spirit. Deep-blue stones are often associated with loyalty and high ideals.

Sapphire

Geology: Sapphire is a variety of corundum, which is the second-hardest known mineral, in the same family as ruby. Mostly known as a source of rich blue stones, sapphire can also be found in other shades like pink, gold, white, or even black. Star sapphires contain needles of rutile that reflect a six-pointed star in bright light. Most sapphires have been heat-treated to deepen the color. Generally, sapphires are cut in oval or rounded rectangular forms to display their blue hues.

Sources: Historically, Myanmar and Kashmir are the most famous sapphire producers. However, Sri Lanka produces most of the stones found today, ranging from pale sky-blue to rich, deep shades.

Sapphires have been cut and set in fine jewelry for hundreds of years. Here, diamonds set off an amazing large stone.

Deep-blue sapphire is a very "royal" shade of blue. It is a favorite stone for engagement rings.

History: Traditionally, sapphire was seen as a symbol of fidelity, making it a favorite for engagement rings. It also has an extensive history as a jewel of royalty and high priesthood. The British Crown Jewels contain very large sapphires of "royal" blue.

Healing uses: Blue sapphire connects you to your highest ideals and spiritual essence. It enables you to communicate your own inner truth. Let the color guide you to your own path of awareness. In healing, sapphire may be applied to the forehead to bring emotional balance and guide your thoughts to the present moment. Sapphire is also said to strengthen the kidneys and the heart.

Lapis Lazuli

Geology: Lapis lazuli is made up of the blue mineral lazurite with golden strands or microcrystals of pyrite and white calcite. The color of lapis lazuli is always deep blue, and the pyrite crystals help to distinguish it from its cousin sodalite, which is also blue but lacks the pyrite. Lapis tends to be opaque in character. It is porous and should be cleaned only with warm soapy water. It is also fairly brittle and needs careful storage.

Lapis lazuli is a deep-blue stone with gold and white strands running through it.

Sources: Lapis lazuli has been mined for over 6,000 years. Afghanistan is an ancient source still used today. Lapis is also mined in Chile, the USA, Siberia, and Myanmar.

History: The tomb of Tutankhamun yielded up many astonishing treasures, most notably the famous mask of the young king fashioned in gold and lapis lazuli. The Pharaohs were adorned with the stone in life and death. In medieval and Renaissance paintings, enameling, and stained glass, particularly rich shades of blue were obtained by using lapis lazuli ground to a powder.

Healing uses: Lapis lazuli assists with spiritual purification, turning the mind away from earthly concerns. It links you to your higher guidance and opens your inner awareness. With its golden pyrite inclusions, it activates the fire of spiritual illumination, especially if placed on the forehead over the third eye. It is said to bring strength and vitality to the whole body.

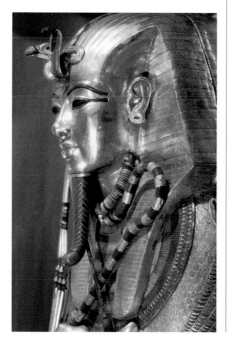

Superb jewelry and gold funeral masks inlaid with lapis adorned the body of the young boy king Tutankhamun.

Violet

Purple and violet shades are beneficially stimulating to the brain—as a mixture of energizing red and cooling blue, they bring wisdom into action.

Amethyst

Geology: Amethyst is purple quartz that can occur in many forms, ranging from tiny crystals to points, clusters, and geodes, which are rocks with inner cavities of varying sizes where the crystals grow inward. Large geodes are sometimes displayed cut open to show the amethyst formations. Amethyst varies in color from dark purple to paler lavender shades.

Small amethyst tumblestones are easy to carry with you when you need them.

traditionally wear amethyst rings. The stone has long had a religious connection and it is found decorating many churches and cathedrals.

Sources: Amethyst is found in Brazil, Uruguay, Bolivia, and Argentina, and Namibia, Zambia, and other African countries. The Ural Mountains in Russia produce very fine amethysts cut for jewelry.

History: The Russian monarch Catherine the Great was passionate about amethysts, and there are also many examples found in the British Crown Jewels. Bishops

If you meditate with amethyst, the energy of the stone can clear the whole body.

Healing uses: Amethyst is one of the most popular stones for healing. It will help you to feel spiritually open and aware, purifying and cleansing your energies on physical, mental, emotional, and spiritual levels. Placed either on the forehead or above the crown of the head, amethyst energy feels like a shower of cool gentle rain through the whole body. Amethyst can also be used to shield you from negativity.

Iolite

Iolite shimmers with its own special reflections. It makes really stunning jewelry.

Geology: Iolite is a violet variety of the mineral cordierite, which can also be found in brown or black shades. In the past, iolite was sometimes known as water sapphire because of its beautiful violet-blue hues. It makes very attractive jewelry. Its structure creates a display called pleochroism, where reflections of violet, clear, and golden lights appear from different angles within the same stone, making a shimmering effect.

Sources: Iolite deposits are found in many parts of the world, including Sri Lanka, India, Mozambique, Madagascar, Brazil, and Myanmar.

History: The Vikings obtained iolite from sources in Norway and Greenland and used thin pieces of the stone as lenses to look up at the sun so they could navigate successfully. The name iolite comes from *ios*, the Greek word for violet.

Healing uses: Iolite can be used to focus your meditation on higher dimensions of spirituality. As human beings, we have the capacity to connect with much wider energies than we are aware of in our everyday life. Awareness of our true spiritual home can help us to behave more responsibly and caringly in the physical world. Iolite can be placed above the crown of the head when lying down to meditate or to receive healing. Iolite is also used when trying to balance the energies of the physical body.

The Vikings used iolite that was found in Norway and Greenland.

Pink

Shades of pink are linked to gentle feelings of unconditional love, and are soothing to the eye and nurturing to the spirit. Pink stones are attractive against all skin types.

Rose Quartz

Geology: Titanium and iron traces give rose quartz its pink color. It occurs in massive pieces and rarely in well-formed crystals. Brazilian rose quartz is used for carving figurines, spheres, and obelisks. In jewelry, the preferred way of presenting rose quartz is as cabochons, smooth, rounded stones polished to show the fine pink shade. A rare variety contains golden threads of rutile, giving a sparkling pink appearance.

Sources: Brazil is a main producer of massive rose quartz slabs, as well as flat-faced crystals. India, Madagascar, and the USA are other notable sources.

History: Rose quartz is very popular with mineral collectors and is also one of the favorite stones of New Age healers.

Healing uses: Rose quartz brings you a gentle sense of

Soft rose quartz has a gentle effect on the body and mind.

warmth and well-being in the heart. It is a good stone to have beside your bed if you have difficulty sleeping or if you feel anxious. It soothes physical, emotional, and environmental stress. It helps balance the emotional and sexual energies, clearing anger, jealousy, or misunderstanding. Meditation with rose quartz brings emotional clarity and peace and the return of a childlike trust. Rose quartz is often placed over the center of the chest in healing sessions to balance the energies of the heart.

Rose quartz connects you to unconditional love.

Jackie Kennedy had an outstanding jewelry collection and was particularly attracted to the lavender-pink hues of kunzite.

Kunzite

Geology: Kunzite is a very attractive lavender-pink stone, formed from lithium aluminium silicate, a pink variety of spodumene. Like iolite, kunzite is pleochroic, meaning that it will show different shades of pink and violet when turned in the light. Although it is as hard as quartz, it is a challenge for gem cutters to bring out all the pink delicacy of this stone, as it can break easily if struck in the wrong direction. It is often found with beryl and tourmaline.

Sources: Kunzite was first discovered in Connecticut, then commercially extracted in California. Today Brazil, Madagascar, and Afghanistan produce most of the gems on the market.

History: Kunzite was named after a famous gemologist and scholar called George Kunz, who was a gem buyer for Tiffany & Co. in the early twentieth century. Kunz was a collector not just of stones but also of legends about gems and jewels.

Healing uses: The combination of violet, a deeply spiritual hue, and pink, relating to the heart, makes kunzite a useful stone for helping you connect to the wider perspective of love as the creative energy behind all things. It can be placed on the chest area in tandem with a rose quartz crystal to support and expand the energy of the heart.

Kunzite has a gentle lavender-pink color, which is very soothing to the eye. It is used to open the heart and its energy.

White

White is a combination of all the colors in the spectrum. Rays of sunlight passing through cut diamonds cause a brilliant rainbow effect. Colorless gems represent unity and perfection.

Diamond

Geology: Diamonds are forever—made of pure carbon, they are the hardest known substance on the Earth, and have the highest melting point and atoms packed more densely than any other mineral. Though they are well known as jewelry, diamonds are also used in industry as excellent electrical insulators. Despite their hardness, they have to be handled very skillfully by jewelers because they will split if they are wrongly struck. They occur in clear, pink, pale yellow, blue, green, reddish, and even black specimens. Diamonds form in pipelike gaps in a host rock called kimberlite.

Exquisitely cut diamonds reflect all the colors of the spectrum.

Sources: Diamonds are found in South Africa, India, Brazil, Russia, Australia, and the USA.

History: There are many famous diamond stories. When the world's largest diamond, the 3,106-carat Cullinan, was discovered in South Africa in 1905, workers were seen to play with it like a lump of glass at the edge of a mine shaft. The Cullinan was presented to King Edward VII on his sixty-sixth birthday and was cut up into four diamonds that now form part of the British Crown Jewels.

Healing uses: Diamond brings out your unique qualities. This aspect is at the root of its use in rings to mark engagements and long marriages. It is a master healer, activating the purest energy all around and within.

The energy of diamonds is said to bring out your own unique personality.

Clear Quartz

Fine quartz clusters form in a huge variety of shapes and sizes.

Geology: Quartz is one of the most common minerals found in the Earth's crust. It is found in countless varieties of clusters, points, masses, colors, and forms. Clear quartz is also known as rock crystal. Though the stone may be cloudy white, the best quality points are completely clear with an icelike appearance. These stones are well defined, and may be single- or double-terminated. Clear quartz with tiny golden needles of rutile is also called rutilated quartz.

Sources: Brazil, the USA, and Africa are among the main sources of the better quality clear quartz.

History: The original meaning of the word "crystal," usually applied to quartz, is from the Greek word for "frozen." Clear quartz is the original crystal ball, with its patterns and milky inclusions providing inspiration for seers. In South America and other locations around the world, large lumps of clear quartz have been found carved into the shape of crystal skulls by ancient peoples.

Healing uses:

Clear quartz is one of the most commonly used stones in healing. It helps to focus and amplify physical, mental, and emotional energy. Quartz points can be placed on any areas of the body that need energizing. Quartz can also be used protectively in challenging environments. Rutilated quartz eases depression and clears negativity.

Quartz crystals are shown here growing into the available space. Stones like these are often cut in half and polished.

B l a c k

Black absorbs all colors within it, like the rainbow sheen of a starling's wing feathers. Black simply holds all the colors of the spectrum in density. Rather than being negative, black stones have mystery in their depths.

Obsidian

Geology: Obsidian is a glassy-textured silicon dioxide, formed from rapidly cooled volcanic lava. Iron and magnesium give the stone its black or very dark green color. Bubbles of long-trapped air may create rainbow or golden reflections. A particularly attractive form of the stone is snowflake obsidian, which contains white speckled inclusions of cristobalite.

Snowflake obsidian is a particularly attractive version of the usual black obsidian.

Sources: Obsidian is found in many states of the USA, such as Arizona, Colorado, and Texas, as well as in Mexico, Italy, and Scotland.

History: Another name for obsidian is "Apache tear," showing its links to the Native American tribes of the southwestern USA. There have been notable archeological finds of ancient arrow heads chipped from obsidian, indicating its use in hunting and the tooling of leather for at least 10,000 years.

Healing uses: Obsidian has a strong masculine affinity. It affects the energies of the lower abdomen and the root chakra. Meditating with obsidian activates warrior energy when you face uncertainty. It is a very grounding stone, helping to prepare for action, and is said to disperse fear.

This stone turtle, with the white speckled inclusions of cristobalite, is an example of snowflake obsidian.

Native Americans have been hunting with obsidian-tipped arrows for thousands of years.

Black Tourmaline

Geology: The long rectangular shapes of tourmaline and its varied colors make it one of the most popular stones to collect. It occurs in a range of colors, including black, pink, green, and blue, as well as forms with more than one color, such as "watermelon" with pink inside and green outside. Black tourmaline is called schorl and is the most common opaque form of the stone, very rich in iron. An unusual property of tourmaline is that it can be electrically charged by heating, so one end is positive and the other negative, giving it a kind of magnetic pull. The stone is cut and set in jewelry, carved into figurines, and sometimes mounted in uncut form.

Black tourmaline forms into regular shapes and is very popular to collect.

Sources: Kenya, Madagascar, and other African countries produce the stone, as well as Brazil, Sri Lanka, Pakistan, and the USA.

History: The many colors of tourmaline have made it a favorite with jewel collectors for centuries—the name comes from an old Sinhalese word *turmali*, which means "mixed."

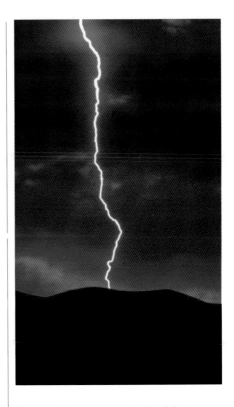

The power of a lightning charge crackles through the air. Tourmaline can be electrically charged by heating.

Healing uses: Black tourmaline has a powerful, dense energy that helps to anchor you if you feel unfocused or pulled in different directions. It has a strong protective influence, which can help you when you are emotionally or physically vulnerable. It strengthens and vitalizes you and makes you aware of the electromagnetic energies of the Earth. It can be placed on the base of the spine to help stabilize and "root" your energies.

Brown

Brown is the color associated with earth, the soil, the dense matter from which all growing things take root; it has a comforting and centering energy. Brown stones are regarded as "grounding" in healing work.

Smoky Quartz

Geology: Smoky quartz is the brown or black variety of quartz, which is thought to have undergone exposure to radiation during its formation. Smoky quartz is often found in granite rocks that still show a tiny amount of natural radioactivity. Most smoky quartz has been heat-treated to deepen the color even more. It is often carved into spheres, pyramids, eggs, and figurines. Smoky quartz forms well-defined six-sided points and is a mineral as hard as clear quartz. Some specimens also contain golden needles of rutile.

Smoky quartz occurs in tawny shades of soft brown. It is a very hard mineral.

Sources: The world's largest supplier of smoky quartz is Brazil, with the Cairngorm Mountains in Scotland, Colorado in the USA, and the Swiss Alps also producing fine specimens.

History: Brown stones like smoky quartz were popular in jewelry in the 1920s and 1930s, particularly in brooches and pendants of neo-Celtic designs.

Healing uses: Smoky quartz helps to strengthen and ground your energies and clear away negativity. Meditation with the stone helps to transform turbulent emotions. It can help to build sexual vitality when used on the lower abdomen and the base of the spine. If you work on a computer, smoky quartz protects against electromagnetic radiation— place a piece on top of your monitor.

All brown crystals remind us that we come from the Earth, and have a positive grounding effect on the body.

Tiger's Eye

Geology: Tiger's eye is
a variety of chalcedony,
which is quartz containing
tiny microcrystals. It is made up
of lustrous brown and yellow fibers in
layers that reflect the light in an unusual
way, causing a phenomenon called
"chatoyancy" (like a cat's eye) when the
stone is moved from side to side. It is
normally found in shades of brown and
gold. However, blue varieties also exist and
some heat-treated specimens may have a
reddish tinge. Tiger's eye is very attractive
when cut and polished in cabochons, smooth,
rounded shapes that demonstrate the
chatoyancy more clearly.

Because of its fibers, tiger's eye shimmers with a luminous glow. This looks best when it is carved into cabochon shapes.

Sources: Large deposits are found in
Myanmar, India, Australia, and South Africa.

History: In medieval times, tiger's eye was
often used as a protection against the evil eye.

Healing uses: With a combination of earthy
brown and radiant gold shades, tiger's eye is
useful to help spirit into matter, bringing ideas
into reality. When you embark on a new path
of expansion, it stabilizes you and makes sure
you that have your feet on the ground. It is
thought to be a relaxing and calming stone,
which can be helpful for inducing sleep. Used
over the solar plexus or the abdomen, it helps
to balance and harmonize both physical and
emotional energies.

Use tiger's eye to relax and calm your mind. It is a stone with very calming energies.

Iridescent

Iridescence is not so much a color as a quality, a sudden appearance of shimmering colors as light moves over a surface. Iridescent stones have long been regarded as having magical properties.

Labradorite

Geology: The beautiful mineral labradorite may show iridescent flashes in a whole variety of shades across its surface—deep blue, violet, green, gold, and orange. It is quite dull in appearance until light plays upon it in the right direction. The effect is caused by different intergrowing layers in its structure, which reflect light waves back against each other, creating the play of colors. Labradorite with many thin layers will show the best effects. As a mineral, it is a variety of feldspar, and forms in chunks embedded in host rocks.

Sources: It is mostly found in Labrador, Canada—from where it gets its name—and also in Scandinavia, where it is sold under the name "spectrolite." Some deposits occur in the USA and Russia.

History: The beautiful variety of colors and changing appearance of labradorite have caused it to be used as a magical talisman since ancient times.

Healing uses: Labradorite reminds you of the changing nature of life moment by moment. Flashes of deep blue within the stone help you to recall that spirit is behind and within all matter. Labradorite expands the third eye and the crown, opening you up to deeper perceptions of reality, and encouraging you to see with new eyes. Its gently shimmering colors may also help to bring you interesting dreams.

Shimmering labradorite displays many hues. It can bring you vivid dreams and enable you to see beyond reality.

Opal

Geology: Opals are not true crystals. Classed as mineraloids, they have a unique structure. They formed millions of years ago as a solution that settled in the cracks and layers of sedimentary rocks, and opals still contain between 6 and 10 percent water. Packed with minuscule spheres of silicon and oxygen molecules, opals flash with many tiny shimmering rainbows as light bounces in these microscopic spaces—the effect is known as "opalescence." The stone's background may be clear, milky white, pale yellow, black, or even the orange-red that is found in fire opals. Black opals contain the brightest colors and are also the most expensive.

Sources: Ancient opal came from mines in Eastern Europe, but for the past one hundred years the main producer has been Australia. Fire opals are found in Mexico and in the state of Oregon.

History: Few stones have had such a varied and fascinating history as opals. There have been many archeological finds of opal artifacts that are thousands of years old. Opals were adored by the ancient Romans; used as an eye tonic in the Middle Ages; celebrated by

Opals look very good in simple jewelry settings and look particularly attractive when they are set in rings.

Shakespeare; and were a favorite gemstone of Queen Victoria.

Healing uses: Opal is alive with gentle shimmers of iridescent color. The most common background is a milky white. This makes the stone very much in tune with the third eye and the crown chakras. The stone can be used to enhance psychic awareness as well as energizing all levels and areas of the body, because of the rainbow of colors that is contained within it.

Opals shimmer with their own beautiful rainbow colors. They can be used to energize the whole of the body.

Gold

Gold as a color ray is radiant, and as warm and bright as the sun itself. The precious metal has been treasured as a setting for gemstones and jewels since the beginning of humankind, and gold minerals are strongly attractive.

The Metal Gold

The hues of the metal gold have mesmerized humankind for thousands of years.

Geology: Gold is a rare metal. Its chemical symbol is Au, which comes from *aurum*, the Latin word for gold. Gold is soft enough to be beaten into fine leaves, and about 1 ounce (28 grams) can make a gold wire about 50 miles (80 kilometers) in length. Its purity is measured in carats, a word derived from Italian, Greek, and Arabic words for carob seeds, which balanced the scales in ancient trading practices. Pure gold is 24 carat. Yellow gold blended with copper is known as red gold, and with platinum, white gold.

Sources: Today, gold is extensively mined in California, Mexico, Colorado, and Canada.

History: Examples of gold jewelry date back thousands of years. The art of smelting and working gold produced amazing Egyptian, Sumerian, and South American artifacts. It has traditionally been a symbol of nobility and royalty. The would-be conquerors of the New World sought El Dorado, the fabled city made entirely of gold.

Healing uses: Gold is seen as cleansing to the whole body, but particularly to the brain and the nervous system. Wearing gold helps to attract positive energy and abundance. In medicine, gold is used to treat rheumatoid arthritis, ulcers, and certain types of cancer, and to repair damaged tissues in surgery.

Pure gold in bars is one of the most valuable commodities to be found. It is immediately associated with wealth and power.

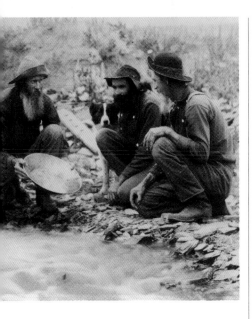

Pyrite is twice as hard as gold and cannot be worked in the same way, although the variety from Italy can be faceted for jewelry.

Sources: Significant quantities of pyrite have been found in the states of Missouri and Illinois. Other sources have also been discovered in South Africa, Peru, Germany, Russia, Italy, and Spain.

History: Although the mineral has a high iron content, pyrite has never been used as a source of iron. However, during World War II, pyrite was mined as a source of sulfur for industrial purposes. Any jewelry that is labeled as marcasite is in fact more likely to be pyrite, because marcasite slowly deteriorates over time.

Early gold panners often mistook pyrite for gold. Although it looks very similar, pyrite has to be worked in a different way.

Pyrite

Geology: Pyrite is a beautiful mineral with a yellow sheen like brass. It is also known as "fool's gold" because it has often been mistaken for the real thing. It is very common and forms opaque crystals with precise, geometric, often cuboid formations. It has a high percentage of iron and sulphur in its composition. Pyrite has the same chemistry as marcasite, and the two are difficult to distinguish from each other.

Healing uses: Pyrite is seen as an overall cleanser of the body, and if brought into your environment it helps to dispel negativity and clear your electromagnetic field. Place it on your desk when working to improve your energy levels. In healing, pyrite can be placed at the base of the spine or on the lower abdomen to boost your energy.

Pyrite has a different sheen from gold—it is paler and looks more like brass.

Silver

The changing energy of the silver ray is like the moon shining on water, delicate and pure, with a fluidity that is cooling and soothing to the senses. Silver as a metal and silver-gray stones have a subtle sheen against the skin.

The Metal Silver

Geology: Silver is a metal with the symbol Ag for *argentum*, the Latin word for silver. It can occur alone in nature and is also often found with gold, copper, or mercury deposits. It is extremely soft, like gold, and is the most electrically and thermally conductive metal, making it very useful in the photographic, watch-making, and computer industries. It can be drawn without breaking into fine wire the thickness of human hair. Fine silver is 999 parts per thousand pure; most jewelry is set in sterling silver, which is 925 parts silver with 75 parts copper.

The soft silver glow of moonlight encases the Earth in a silver radiance. Silver connects you to this moon energy.

Red-hot silver ore pours into a waiting mold. Like gold, silver is extremely soft and can be worked very easily.

Sources: Silver is widely distributed all over the globe. The most notable deposits today are situated in Mexico, Canada, and in the state of Arizona.

History: Many examples of stunning silver jewelry and artifacts can be found in ancient Celtic, Roman, and Indian civilizations. Silver has often been associated with the moon because of its silvery shimmer.

Healing uses: The energy of silver is cool, as opposed to the bright radiance of gold. Silver is subtle, seen as linked to the unconscious, bringing intuitive impulses. Silver connects you with your dream-self, the part of you that is mysterious and knowing.

Hematite has an attractive mat sheen to it. It is used to warm and strengthen blood circulation and increase physical energy.

Hematite

Geology: Hematite is iron oxide, a mineral that is a source of opaque, silver-gray crystals. The host rock and its dust are blood-red in color, providing a natural source of red pigment. Hematite may form crystals in a number of shapes and masses—rounded kidney-shaped stones as well as bladed crystals can be found.

Sources: Notable specimens can be found in the Lake District in northern England, Mexico, Brazil, Australia, and Canada.

History: In ancient times, the red rocks of hematite were said to be formed from the blood of warriors who died in battle. The word "hematite" comes from the Greek root *haem*, which refers to the blood. Traditionally it was held by women in childbirth. For centuries and even until recently, finely ground particles of red hematite dust were used in make-up formulations as blusher!

Healing uses: Hematite is a grounding and strengthening stone, which helps to center you very much in the body, particularly when your energies are overstretched. It has a calming and soothing effect on the nerves. It can be worn to strengthen courage and energy when facing difficult challenges. Hematite also counteracts negative energy in your environment, for example when placed near a computer. In healing, it is considered to balance blood circulatio

Hematite powder is blood-red and is therefore used in healing work to treat blood disorders and the circulatory system.

Simple Crystal Healing Methods

Working with crystal energies involves fine-tuning your intuition and sensitivity to your environment. You can use the chart on page 145, or choose a crystal from the Crystal Index because of its colors or associations. Alternatively, you can simply work with a stone because you feel that it is the right one for you.

What is Healing?

The word "healing" is derived from an old Germanic root *hael*, which can mean "complete," "whole," or even "holy." It is a process by which the body, mind, and spirit are gently balanced to bring a sense of wholeness, oneness with all life. Anyone can benefit from

Crystals can be hung on a chain so that you can use them as pendulums for dowsing work.

Gently laying a crystal over your heart area can soothe any troubled emotions.

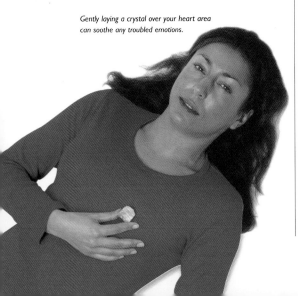

healing, provided they are open to receiving it. If you have complex physical problems or deep emotional issues, you are advised to seek the help of a suitably qualified practitioner. For general balancing and opening your own awareness, you can benefit from working on yourself. After any exercises, it is useful to make notes or drawings you can come back to at a later date—healing is an ever-unfolding process.

Using a Pendulum

A pendulum can be made of a balanced quartz or cut-glass point suspended on a chain or a string. Dowsing, as this is called, is an ancient art. If you hold the pendulum still and say your real name, it should respond by turning clockwise. If you say a false name, it should swing from side to side or counterclockwise. With practice, you will get used to how your pendulum shows "yes" and "no." You can then sit and touch each chakra area from base to crown with one hand, asking if that level needs energy, and watching the pendulum swing in response. You can also simply hold the pendulum over a stone and ask if it is the right one to use at this time.

Working with a Single Crystal

Prepare your space: clear away everyday clutter, then light a candle and perhaps some incense. Select a suitable stone for yourself—by intuition, dowsing, or by consulting the chart or Crystal Index—and sit quietly holding it in your hands. Breathe deeply and relax. Take your awareness into your body and note any tensions. Using your breath, simply dissolve them like clouds in a blue sky. Then take your awareness to your stone—to its color, shape, and feeling in your hands. Relax and see what impressions or feelings come to you for a few minutes. To come out of the process, take a few deep breaths and gently stretch your arms and hands.

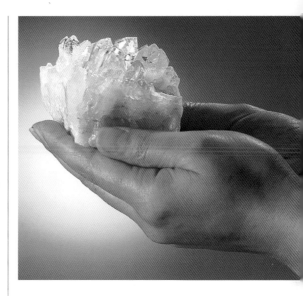

Holding a crystal in your hands can help to fine-tune your intuition. What exactly are you expecting from this mineral?

Using Crystals on the Body

Lie down comfortably on a mat on the floor. Place a piece of rose quartz over your heart and then relax, slowly breathing away any tension in your body. Silently and gently focus your intention on opening and expanding the energies in your heart chakra. Breathe into the heart area and visualize the rose quartz crystal shining the light of unconditional love into your whole being. Now visualize that rosy ray expanding beyond you to include all life forms. To end the exercise, take a few slow, deep breaths and then flex your fingers and toes before slowly getting up.

Living With Crystals

Crystals can play a vital part in making your environment beautiful wherever you are. You may choose them for their beauty, or for a particular function that is relevant to you or your living space. Here are some ideas for placing and using crystals in your space.

Bedroom

It is worth saying here that too many crystals in the bedroom may not be such a good idea: you mostly want to relax and sleep in there, so too many amplified energies may not help! Having said that, stones like tiger's eye, amethyst, and rose quartz are said to be gentle and restful to have around you, perhaps at your bedside. If you want to enhance the energy for love-making, don't forget Cleopatra's favorite green stones like peridot or the expansive warm energy of amber. In a child's bedroom, a gentle blue stone like celestite brings a sense of peace and calm.

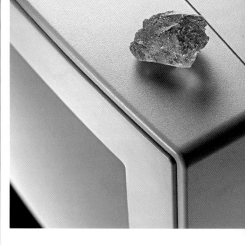

Try placing a crystal on your computer monitor to balance your environment and disperse negative energies.

Study or Office

Here electromagnetic radiation from computers is the main issue. Stones like smoky quartz or amethyst can be used to help maintain a balanced environment. Try placing a stone on top of your monitor. If you are to have a meeting you feel may be challenging, you can place a large piece of rose quartz in the middle of the table to calm the energies. If you need inspiration, a beautiful clear quartz cluster is a wonderful,

Focusing on your chosen crystals can help clear away negativity and generate new ideas. Remember that stones constantly used for this need regular cleansing.

complex, light-filled shape to concentrate on, clearing your mind for new ideas. Stones that sit constantly in an electronic environment will need regular cleansing.

Bathroom

It can be very restful to put little smooth polished crystals in the bath with you. Water is a great conductor, so the bath will be gently energized by them—and so will you. Rose quartz, carnelian, citrine, amethyst, or tiger's eye are fun to try. Place the crystals in the bath and run the water, adding three to four drops of an essential oil like lavender or frankincense, then light a candle on the window sill and lie back for a lovely mystical soak.

Crystals really come into their own when they are placed in water. Try bathing with crystals in the bath for a really restful soak.

Combine crystals, fresh flowers, and candles to create a beautiful and uplifting living space.

Living Room

Here you may wish to create a special space for your crystals. A good idea is to set aside a particular table covered with a silk cloth, with a beautiful candle in a holder, a vase for fresh flowers, and an incense holder, as well as your stones. In India, and other countries, many houses have their own small shrines, which are tended daily. A beautiful arrangement of crystals, candles, and fresh flowers is an attractive focal point and helps to provide a wonderful energy in your living room. Even the intrusive presence of a television set can be enhanced by an amethyst cluster placed on it, which helps balance electromagnetic rays as well.

Meditating With Crystals

Meditation is a way of accessing a state of deep stillness, which is health-giving in this fast-moving modern age. In a meditative state, you experience deep peace and relaxation. This lets your body restore itself on a cellular level, and your mind and spirit be regenerated.

Meditation aims to create in your mind the stillness and peace that is found in nature. It can be very energizing.

Making Time and Creating Space

Meditation is not "doing nothing," it is giving yourself time to just "be," releasing yourself from daily demands for a short and beneficial time. Try to arrange a regular 15-minute slot each day for yourself and see how it works for you.

Crystals as a Focus

For meditation, crystals can be contemplated as a fixed object, held in the hands, or placed on the body. To develop the earlier exercises, you can add in visualization, letting the

power of your creative imagination and intuition respond to the crystal. After these exercises, try writing notes or drawing your experiences and keep them as a reference.

Clear Quartz Exercise: Inner Cleansing

Using a clear quartz cluster or point, sit holding the crystal in your hands. Breathe deeply and release all tension from your body for a few moments. Now imagine a fountain of white light that begins just above the crown of your head and enters

Sit and relax, letting your creative imagination run free. If you also hold your crystal, you can let your imagination work on that too.

Use a crystal that feels right to you at the time. You will know instinctively which one is meant for you.

your skull, flowing down your face, neck, back, shoulders, arms, and hands and into your crystal. As the energy builds in the crystal, let it flow on down your abdomen, hips, and legs and into the Earth. Thank the Earth for her gifts. Imagine yourself to be a conduit between Earth and Heaven. To end the exercise, breathe deeply and flex your feet and hands.

Amber Exercise: Connecting to the Plant Kingdom

Amber is an organic gemstone made up of fossilized tree resin, often containing tiny pollen grains or other ancient life forms. For this exercise, take a piece of amber with you on a walk. If possible, find a tall pine tree, or if none is nearby, let your intuition guide you to a tree. Stand with your back to the trunk and hold the amber in your hands. Breathe deeply and feel the upright strength of the tree. Imagine you are drawing warm earth energy up though your feet, your legs, hips, abdomen, and into the amber in your hands. Let the energy continue flowing up through your back, heart, shoulders and up out of your

head, up the tree, and out into the universe. Relax and feel yourself to be a part of all Nature. Breathe deeply and stretch your arms to come out of the exercise—and thank the tree for letting you do this.

You can work with any stones that seem appropriate to you—with time, you will develop your own favorites. Try to be aware and thankful at all times for the gifts of the mineral kingdom and the Earth.

All stones, minerals, and precious gems come from the Earth. Try to remember this at all times.

Buying Crystals

Obtaining crystals for your collection can be a lot of fun; however, a little preparation is a good idea. Use these guidelines to help you make informed and appropriate choices so you are happy with your purchases and feel they are right for you.

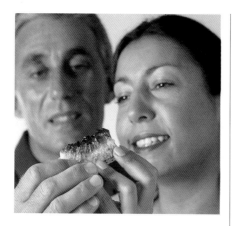

Buy your crystals from a supplier who will give you helpful advice and important information.

Today crystals are widely available from a variety of sources. You can buy inexpensive stones that are both esthetically appealing and are useful for healing purposes.

Finding a Supplier

When you are buying crystals, it really helps to do your research. Your local telephone directory may contain listings of crystal stores and outlets. If you know a crystal healing practitioner, ask them where they source their stones—perhaps they will sell to you. The main thing is, visit as many of these people and places as you can. Feel the atmosphere: are the stones housed and displayed with care? If you ask questions (as you should), are you given helpful answers and advice? Many stones on the market are heat-treated, dyed, or grown artificially in a laboratory. Ask the supplier where their stones come from. If they are unwilling to discuss it, think twice about buying. Many fairs and trade shows supply crystals, and the same guidelines apply here. Get to know your retailer and trust your intuition. There are mail order crystal companies, but the disadvantage is that you do not see or handle the stones before you buy. Your personal experience of the stones is important, particularly if you want them for healing work.

Try out crystals in the store and feel which ones are right for you. This is a vital part of buying your stones.

Natural minerals can be collected from beaches or other locations. Be sure that you have permission to do this.

Collecting Crystals

Mineral collecting is a popular hobby. Even collecting stones from the beach or rivers is a fun pastime. Your local museum may know of a geological group who go out collecting, and it is a wonderful experience to see rocks in veins in a natural setting. If you live in a granite area, for example, it will be possible to find stones with small quartz crystals embedded in them. It is best to join a group so that you do not get into trouble for trespassing or for doing any environmental damage.

Buying for Other People

Some crystal healing books suggest you should choose your own stones rather than choose them for other people—again, because of the personal interaction between the holder and the stone. To choose for someone, you really need to ask your intuition, visualize the person, and ask if the stone is right for them.

The beauty and variety of crystals means that you will always find something to suit your purpose and your price range.

Birthstone List

This may also help when choosing crystals for other people. Birthstone lists became very popular in the eighteenth and nineteenth centuries and do vary, but here is a general selection.

January	garnet
February	amethyst
March	aquamarine
April	diamond
May	tourmaline
June	moonstone
July	carnelian
August	peridot
September	lapis lazuli
October	opal
November	topaz
December	turquoise

Glossary

Here is a list of terms that occur in the text with explanations.

Cabochon

a gem cut and polished into a smooth, domed shape.

Chakra

an energy center in the body.

Chatoyancy

a shimmering light-effect like a cat's eye, e.g. in tiger's eye.

Cleansing

the practice of cleaning crystals physically and energetically.

Conductor

an agent that permits the free flow of heat or electricity.

Crystal

a mineral with a precise geometrically arranged structure.

Element

one of the basic building blocks of matter, e.g. carbon or hydrogen.

Face

one of the sides of a crystal.

Geode

a hollow lump of rock with crystals growing inward.

Geology

the science of the history and development of the Earth and its minerals.

Inclusion

specks, bubbles, or other minerals showing up in crystals.

Inorganic

a substance of inert origin like a mineral.

Iridescence

a shimmering, multicolored play of light.

Magma

molten rock at the Earth's core.

Mineral

a natural inorganic chemical compound.

Molten

melted or in liquid form, e.g. volcanic lava.

Nodule

a small lump of rock.

Opalescence

a milky, soft, luminous sheen, as in opals.

Organic

a substance with a plant or animal origin.

Programing

conscious intent directed into a crystal for healing purposes.

Rutile

strands of golden mineral appearing in clear quartz and other stones.

Setting

the art of placing gemstones in precious metal.

Termination

the pointed end of a crystal.

Tumblestones

small, smooth, crystal pebbles rounded off in a machine.

Useful Addresses and Websites

USA

The Crystalis Institute
440 Bayley Hazen Road, Walden,
Vermont
www.crystalisinstitute.com
Set up by Naisha Ahsian in the USA and offers
courses in crystal healing.

Association of Melody Crystal Healing
www.taomchi.com
Information on crystology, crystal healing,
courses, and instructors.

United Kingdom

The International Association of Crystal Healing Therapists (IACHT)
PO Box 344, Manchester, M60 2EZ, UK
www.iacht.co.uk

The IACHT publishes a list of accredited therapists in the UK and details of training in crystal healing.

The European College of Vibrational Medicine

Unity, Hall Green, Rectory Road, Gissing, Diss, Norfolk, IP22 5UX, UK

Tel: +44 (0) 1379 677869

www.raven.org.uk

An online distance learning college with courses on crystal healing.

The Internet is full of amazing and informative websites on crystals. Here are a few:

International Colored Gemstone Association

www.gemstone.org

Geological information

www.mineralgalleries.com

www.nationalgeographic.com (good for superb photographic material)

www.nhm.ac.uk (The Natural History Museum, London, UK)

home remedies

Introduction

In the old days, when you had a sore throat your first reaction was probably not to call out the doctor but to head for the kitchen cabinet. There you would find the honey jar, spoon a liberal portion into some boiling water, add the juice and rind of two or three lemons and sip the warming concoction slowly. Honey and lemon is one of the best known and best loved home remedies and is still used today as a basis for many of the most famous over-the-counter medicines and throat pastilles.

Nowadays, however, new technology and increasingly sophisticated medical advances have all but banished the old-fashioned home remedy to the archives of history. Most are dismissed as "old wives' tales" and yet many of these ancient remedies have been the subject of rigorous clinical trials. The humble garlic, for example, has probably been the subject of more scientific studies than any

A cupful of honey, lemon, and hot water will help to ease the symptoms of a cold such as sore throat.

other herb. We now know it is excellent for thinning blood, lowering cholesterol levels, and even curing the common cold. It is marketed as the new cure-all for myriad complaints.

Modern drugs can be life savers but they often have too many side effects to warrant their use for every little sniffle or stomach upset. Home and herbal remedies tend to heal without suppressing symptoms, and used in the correct dosage are perfectly safe and have no side effects. Herbs are easy to find and can be used in cooking or in salads. Some, which you can grow in your garden, can be ground up and used as inhalants or to perfume a bath. Others—which are more likely to be in your

The modern herb garden can provide many home remedy possibilities. Herbs can be added to food or used as a treatment.

kitchen—can be added to cooking or made up into poultices and muscle rubs.

As the methods of testing the compounds contained in many natural remedies become more sophisticated, many cynics are beginning to sit up and take notice. And as more and more of our so-called "wonder drugs" prove only to suppress symptoms rather than get to the root cause, it is little wonder that more and more people are now looking for a healthier option for everyday complaints. The beauty of home remedies is that they are accessible and easy to prepare. Many of the remedies contained in this section have been passed down through the generations by word of mouth—others have surpassed all expectations in clinical trials. Some you will remember from the old nursery rhymes. Remember when Jack fell down and broke his crown and Jill fixed it with vinegar and brown paper? It may have sounded a strange remedy for a bad head, but in fact this used to be a remedy for headaches and migraine!

Garlic has been the subject of many scientific studies.

How to Make Home Remedies

Compress

A compress is simply a piece of cloth soaked in a bowl of hot or cold herbal extract. It eases the strain of painful joints and muscles and can help to soothe skin rashes. Almost any herbs can be applied as a compress if you need to treat a problem locally. All you need to do is soak a piece of cheesecloth or lint in the herbal infusion of your choice and apply it to the affected area, renewing it as and when necessary.

Steam Inhalation

For steam inhalations, which are best for stressed or inflamed lungs, make up an infusion of the herb you want to use (essential oils can also be used) and add it to a basinful of hot water. Drape a towel around your head and the basin so that you keep the steam in, and inhale slowly and deeply for a few minutes.

Tincture

To make a tincture, put 4½ cups of fresh herbs or 1¾ cups of dried herbs in a jar and add 2¼ cups of vodka (it acts as a preservative). Add a scant cup of water, seal the jar and store in a cool place for 2–3 weeks, checking and shaking it occasionally. Strain the liquid through a cheesecloth bag into a pitcher and then into sterilized bottles.

Infusion

To make an infusion to drink hot or cold, warm a teapot and add about ¼ cup of dried herbs or ½ cup of fresh herbs. Pour 2¼ cups of hot water on the herbs. Cover the pot until the herbs have infused (about 10 minutes). Strain the infusion through a plastic tea strainer. Add a little honey or unrefined sugar. Drink a cupful. You can keep the remainder in a pitcher and store in the refrigerator for up to 48 hours.

History of Home Remedies

Home remedies have been around for thousands of years. Even these days about 30 percent of prescription drugs are still synthesized from plants. In fact, the word "drug" comes from an old Dutch word, *drogge*, which means "to dry"—which is how many plant medications were prepared.

Honey is one of the oldest remedies known—in the days of the ancient Egyptians it was used as a remedy for high blood pressure. Honey contains a huge range of vitamins, enzymes, proteins, and amino acids; it can actually be classified as a complete food. Honey not only lowers blood pressure but is also a key factor in transmitting nerve impulses.

Vinegar is another ancient remedy which has stood the test of time. Cider vinegar was used for treating ailments long before the expression "an apple a day keeps the doctor away" was coined. Apples contain pectin—a soluble fiber—as well as all sorts of vitamins and minerals. Cider vinegar is rich in potassium, which promotes cell growth, and for many years vinegar was believed to be the "fountain of youth." It can help high blood pressure and is excellent for curing cramp. Vinegar was also used by the ancient Assyrians to cure earache, and during the American Revolutionary and Civil Wars it was used as both an antiseptic and disinfectant.

The Chinese were big on home remedies and were one of the first civilizations to recognize ginger for its therapeutic properties. It was and still is used to combat nausea, boost the immune system, and reduce inflammation.

The ancient Egyptians used honey for high blood pressure centuries before the full range of its benefits had been scientifically analyzed. It contains a raft of vitamins and may be classified as a complete food. No wonder it is so useful in the battle against colds.

Some of the best home remedies were discovered on the battlefield. Garlic was used to dress wounds in World War I.

For more than 2,000 years celery stalk was a remedy used by Chinese healers to treat high blood pressure. Recent research has shown that celery stalk does contain compounds that reduce high blood pressure by relaxing the smooth muscle lining the blood vessels.

Some of the best home remedies were discovered on the battlefield. During World War I, for example, garlic was pounded in water and applied to wounds on a bed of moss as an accepted field dressing, while during the eighteenth century sailors used to thrust a piece of shag tobacco into a wound to staunch the bleeding!

So you can see that home remedies are an excellent form of first-line treatment. And although this book is not in any way intended to replace the advice of your doctor, by being more aware of the benefits of home remedies

Vinegar has many uses as a natural home remedy. It is rich in potassium and can help with cramp and high blood pressure.

you can begin to understand how to heal yourself.

Naturally, if symptoms persist, or you are in any doubt whatsoever about a health problem, you should always consult a professional. But before you pick up the telephone, you should use this section as a reference point for everything from smelly feet to the common cold. You will be surprised at what may be lurking in your kitchen cabinet that might just do the trick!

China has a long history of natural home remedy use, including celery stalk to reduce high blood pressure.

Burns, Scalds, and Sunburn

Although second- and third-degree burns require hospital treatment, mild first-degree burns are often superficial and can be treated at home. Any burn needs cooling down, so run tepid water directly onto the wound for at least five minutes to reduce the heat and give pain relief. For a chemical burn it is vital to keep flushing the skin with cold running water until well after the pain has subsided. Clean the burn of any grit or dirt very carefully, avoiding breaking the skin or blistered areas.

Remedies for Burns

Plain yogurt applied to a burn will keep it cool, or you can make up a soothing poultice from honey and yogurt. Adding crushed elderberries to the poultice will make it more effective or mash the leaves of the elder with a little butter and use it as a mild cream for the affected area.

Cucumber mashed to a pulp and mixed with glycerine makes a particularly wonderful moisturizing balm.

Cool the whole area with a cider vinegar splash and make sure the person who has been burned has plenty of fluids.

Try making a tea made from lemon balm, which will both calm the patient and provide further pain relief.

Flush the skin with cold running water for a while after a chemical burn—even after the pain has subsided.

Olive oil can bring effective relief to a painful scald.

Remedies for Scalds

Olive oil can bring immediate relief to a painful scald and will improve the chances of healing without blisters or scars. If you have any lavender or peppermint essential oils to hand, add these to the olive oil to help ease the stinging sensation around the wound.

When sunburn spoils a holiday, natural home remedies made from lemon, cold tea, and baking soda can come to the rescue.

Remedies for Sunburn

For instant relief from sunburn, dab on a little lemon juice or soak a flannel in cold tea and place it over the affected area. For the kind of all-over sunburn that keeps you awake at night, try adding two tablespoons of baking soda to a cool bath and immerse your whole body in the water. You can also mash the pulp of a ripe avocado and smooth over the sunburnt area for a soothing effect.

Bathe your face in buttermilk or grate up some potatoes and apply to the sunburned area. The starch will cool and soothe the burn. Use cold peppermint tea as a mild wash to ease the stinging. Or you can try dissolving Epsom salts or baking soda in cold water and draping a cloth soaked in the solution over the affected area.

Milk of magnesia has been successfully used to treat sunburn, and mud or clay can ease the stinging pain.

Remedy for Chapped Skin

Fill a cheesecloth bag full of oats, then tie it up at the top and drop it in a cool bath, or soak it in warm water, squeeze it out and rub it over the chapped area during the day to ease the pain.

A cheesecloth bag filled with oats and soaked in a cool bath can be rubbed over areas of chapped skin to help relieve the pain.

FIRST-AID

Bites and Stings

There is nothing more painful and irritating than being stung by an angry wasp or bitten alive by mosquitoes. It is vital that you have identified what has bitten you before using a home remedy, and if you are traveling abroad and are stung by an unknown flying creature, it is always safest to seek medical advice. However, for the everyday type of insect bite or sting, ice-cold water or witch hazel are good first-line remedies.

Remedies for Bee Stings

Remove bee stings with tweezers (grasp the sting below the poison sac). Apply a paste of baking soda and cold water. A mixture of parsley juice and honey will also help to ease the irritation—crush the parsley leaves and stems to release the juice.

A cold, wet tea bag makes a marvelous poultice for bites and stings. Tea contains tannic acid, which helps to reduce swelling.

It helps to identify what you have been bitten by before using a home remedy.

Remedies for Wasp Stings

Cider vinegar or lemon will help to stop the irritation and itching. In the rare event of swallowing a wasp, drink a glass of cold water mixed with a teaspoon of salt. If you have been stung in the mouth, suck on ice cubes until the pain subsides. Mix cider vinegar with baking soda to make a poultice and apply directly to a bite. A cold, wet tea bag makes a marvelous poultice—the tannic acid helps to reduce swelling. A paste of ground cloves and cold water can also help.

Remedies for Mosquito Bites

Rub neat garlic directly onto mosquito bites to prevent infection—and mosquitoes loathe the smell of garlic, so eat the rest of the clove raw! Honey and baking soda mixed together

The pain of a jellyfish sting can be reduced by pouring seawater over the affected area for at least ten minutes.

can help the itchiness around the bite, or rub the rind of a lemon neat onto the site of the bite. Sprinkle dried lavender along your window sill to stop further attacks—the smell of lavender also instantly repels mosquitoes!

To make another mosquito repellent, tie together some dried lavender, peppermint, and catnip and secure it with a piece of thin wire. Light the bundle and keep it in a jar nearby. The smoke will mask your own smell and literally put the bugs off the scent!

If you are covered in bites, you need to break down the toxins which have been released into your body. Try drinking herb teas made from dandelion root, red clover, or burdock.

Make a tincture of horseradish using half a cup of grated horseradish root and 2½ cups of rubbing alcohol. Steep the root in the alcohol for 2–3 days. Shake the mixture up twice every day. Strain off the grated root and bottle the liquid. You can use the tincture for most bites and stings, minor skin wounds, and any superficial infections.

Parsley juice combined with honey can help to ease the irritation caused by bee stings.

Remedies for Stinging Nettle Stings

Apply the juice from the stems of the nettles. Dock leaves, which often grow nearby, can also be wrapped around the affected area to ease the pain.

Remedies for Jellyfish Stings

Pour seawater over the affected area for ten minutes. The water releases the remaining toxins. Cold cider vinegar, ice, alcohol, or diluted ammonia applied to the sting are all effective.

Cuts and Grazes

Cuts and grazes have a habit of looking far worse than they really are, but once minor injuries are cleaned up, there are several remedies which can be used to help. If a cut is bleeding profusely, elevate the injured part and press a clean cloth directly onto the wound. The most important thing with any cut or graze is to get the affected area as clean as possible before applying any covering.

Remedies for Cuts and Grazes

Wash cuts and grazes with diluted witch hazel to prevent infection. You can also use Friar's balsam or a few drops of calendula in warm water. If none of this is to hand, warm, soapy water with a few drops of lemon juice or a teaspoon of salt added will do the trick. If you are in a remote place, then plain saliva can be a great healer.

Parsley juice or heavy cream can be placed directly onto a wound and covered with a gauze dressing.

Crush up some parsley leaves and apply the juice directly onto a cut or graze.

Change it every two hours to make sure the wound is cleansed efficiently. Try washing the wound with the water from boiled parsnips and apply the warm pulp as a poultice.

Garlic acts as a marvelous natural antiseptic, so make up a mixture of crushed garlic and honey for a healing poultice and apply it directly to cuts and grazes. Use honey neat and cover with a bandage to prevent air or moisture penetrating the wound.

For a gravel graze, apply bread mixed with egg yolk and warm milk directly to the graze in order to gently draw out any small pieces of grit. Mash up raw avocado and cover with sterile gauze to prevent infection and promote healing.

Washing cuts and grazes with witch hazel can help to prevent infection.

Honey is particularly effective at drawing out the tiny pieces of gravel that tend to be found in children's cuts and grazes. Lemon is one of nature's most powerful astringents, so use it raw on cuts and grazes to stop bleeding. It will sting like mad but it really does the trick.

Drinking a cup of peppermint tea will immediately help to clot blood. It is particularly useful for nosebleeds.

Garlic wine made from chopped garlic steeped in white wine for several hours will cleanse and prevent infections in wounds and cuts.

In order to protect the area after cleaning, you should apply a paste of garlic and honey and cover with some fine gauze.

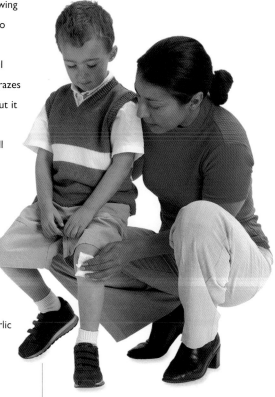

Apply a poultice of bread mixed with egg yolk and warm milk directly to a gravel graze to draw out any small pieces of grit.

You can wash a wound with the water from boiled parsnips and apply the warm pulp as a poultice.

Washing Wounds

Use the following for washing wounds:

- Witch hazel (diluted)
- Friar's balsam (diluted)
- Calendula (diluted)
- Water with salt or drops of lemon juice
- Water in which parsnips have been boiled

FIRST-AID
Bruises, Sprains, and Shock

Old wives used to recommend cold steak be placed directly onto a bruise. Nowadays, ice-cold water is the best cure, or a gentler method is to swab the bruise with a warm compress and massage it gently to stimulate the circulation. Injuries that cause bruises or sprains may lead to shock and even fainting, and caution is needed in these cases.

Remedies for Bruises and Sprains

If you have no ice, try a packet of frozen vegetables. Soak a sprained hand or foot in a bowl of warm water into which you have grated an onion and a potato.

Massaging a bruise or sprain with onion will bring pain relief to the affected area.

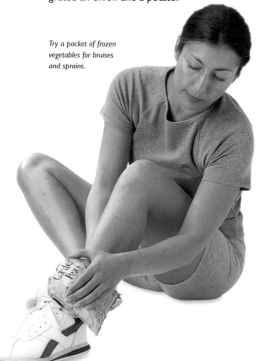

Try a packet of frozen vegetables for bruises and sprains.

Half an onion rubbed on the affected area will quickly soothe it. Black eyes can be miraculously cured with a cold comfrey tea bag placed directly over the offending area. Witch hazel will also help to soothe swellings and also to reduce inflammation and bleeding.

Apply hot or cold compresses of vinegar, particularly the type that is made from astringent fruits, such as raspberry and rose, because they will help to reduce swelling and inflammation.

An old cook's remedy is parsley butter or oats mixed to a paste with boiling water and applied on a cloth to the affected area.

Remedies for Shock

Hot, sweet tea was always thought to be a restorative remedy for shock, and in fact honey added to any hot drink is a great healer. Basil and sage tea sweetened with honey is a great cure for someone who has experienced a mild shock.

Chamomile tea is also useful in this situation because it acts as a gentle sedative and therefore eases tension.

Orange blossom in hot water is believed to relieve anxiety. Not only can it be given to a patient as a kind of infusion, orange blossom water has a further point in its favor; a flannel can be steeped in the liquid to cool a patient down. Its soothing and refreshing properties will help to restore calm.

Cinnamon and honey dissolved in boiling water will help to pep someone up after they have fainted.

Remedies for Fainting

A hot tea made from peppermint, sage, lemon balm, or rosemary will quickly revive someone coming round after fainting. Cinnamon and honey dissolved in boiling water are also good for this. Angelica was believed by ancient wise women to be the elixir of life and can be an excellent tonic.

Caution

- If you receive a blow to the head, it may cause concussion, and you should always be seen by a doctor.

- Any injury that causes bruising or a sprain may also cause shock and fainting.

- There is a big difference between clinical shock, which can kill, and the sort of mild shock people suffer when they receive bad news or minor injuries. Again, it is best to seek medical advice.

Chamomile tea and basil and sage tea are very effective means of restoring calm and will help in the management of shock.

Colds, Flu, and Coughs

Plenty of garlic or the herb echinacea will help boost the immune system and stop colds and flu from getting a hold. If you should be unlucky, however, at the first sign of a cold and fever, make up a mustard footbath by adding one teaspoon of dried mustard to a bowl of very hot water. Mustard has a warming effect and inhaling an infusion will clear phlegm and draw infection and congestion away from the chest.

Remedies for Colds and Flu

Lemon and honey are traditional remedies for colds and flu—lemon because of its high vitamin C content and because it improves the body's ability to expel toxins, and honey because it can help to soothe a sore throat. You could make up a hot drink with the juice of two to four lemons and stir in a dessertspoon of honey for a comforting home remedy.

Add fresh ginger or peppermint, or their essential oils, to a hot bath or footbath. They both help you to perspire, which gets rid of toxins from the body. A ginger footbath also draws away blood from the head to the feet and in this way can reduce the heat congestion you so often feel in the rest of the body when you are suffering from a cold or flu.

Echinacea, available in tablet form, helps to boost the immune system and keep colds and flu at bay.

Garlic is a natural antibiotic and is good for all bronchial problems and lung complaints. If you eat garlic neat, try eating a sprig of parsley or dandelion leaf afterward to freshen your breath.

Onions are excellent for colds. Put a thick slice of onion into boiling water and add half a teaspoon of cayenne pepper. Strain and drink the liquid hot at bedtime.

Pour 2 cups of hot water over a handful of fresh pine needles, put a towel over your head, and inhale the vapors deeply to counteract congestion.

You can even add a little lemon and

Garlic can act as a natural antibiotic and is good for all bronchial problems.

Pine needles can provide relief from chestiness. Pour hot water over some pine needles in a bowl, place a towel over your head and the bowl, and inhale the vapors.

honey to the remaining water and drink it so that you increase your levels of vitamins C and A, which will help to speed up your recovery from illness.

Eat plenty of yogurt, which can kill bacteria on its own. It will also help your body to produce more antibodies that will kill any invading organisms.

Remedies for Coughs

If you have a persistent cough, try a poultice of roasted onion applied to the chest every two hours. Onions can also be drunk as a warm broth to cleanse the airways and to reduce congestion.

Try an infusion of grated fresh ginger root with spices such as cloves and cinnamon to help ease a chesty cough.

In Romany medicine, nettles are believed to rid the lungs and stomach of excess phlegm. For asthma and bronchitis, add a handful of young nettles to 1 cup of boiling water. Strain and drink the juice.

A cabbage leaf poultice works well when the chest is tight from coughing. Cabbage has an extraordinary ability to draw out toxins.

Crush the leaves with a rolling pin until the juice starts to appear. Place three or four leaves over the chest area and cover with gauze. Then place a warm blanket over to keep it in place. You can also drink the juice of the cabbage sweetened with a teaspoon of honey.

If you have a cold, you could try a bedtime drink of onion and cayenne pepper in hot water to soothe the symptoms.

GENERAL AILMENTS
Sore Throat and Fever

At the first signs of a fever, lemon juice and honey or apple cider vinegar and honey diluted in plenty of warm water will help. Cold drinks of lemon juice, lemon barley water, or fresh unsweetened fruit juices are all good remedies and will help to bring a temperature down.

Remedies for a Sore Throat

For a bad sore throat, make up a gargle with either salt, lemon juice, or cider vinegar diluted with warm water. The salt helps to destroy the bacteria that cause the sore throat and helps to relieve the burning sensation. Squeeze the oil of a whole garlic clove into

Salt, lemon juice, or cider vinegar in a glass of warm water makes an effective gargle to ease a sore throat.

Hyssop, a herb belonging to the mint family, can provide a boost to the immune system in the form of a tea or tisane.

a bowl, mix with cayenne pepper and warm salt water, and soak a clean cloth in the liquid. Wear the cloth around your throat for instant relief. Gargling with plain salt water can also be soothing.

Echinacea acts as a natural antibiotic by boosting the body's immune system and fighting infection and illness. Garlic and onions relieve congestion and infections by reducing the amount of mucus in the nasal cavities.

Blackcurrants, crushed up in boiling water, can help your body to fight infection and inflammation.

Try using a cool water compress applied to the legs and feet as a means of calming a fever.

Ancient Remedy for Fever

An ancient remedy for fever involved mixing cloves, cream of tartar, and some cinnamon stick in a little tea with molasses or honey added. If you drank it every day of your life, it was supposed to prevent fevers from occurring!

antioxidants will also help rid the body of free radicals which damage the cells in the body.

Blackcurrants also counter infection and inflammation. Try a spoonful crushed into a cupful of boiling water and left to infuse for ten minutes—sip the drink slowly and chew the fruit. Red sage is the most famous remedy for sore throat—a tea made from the herb and drunk with a dash of cider vinegar will work wonders.

There is also a variety of teas and tisanes that help the immune system fight back. Some of the best remedies include hyssop, a member of the mint family. Lemon, which contains vitamin C, and any tea that contains

Boil angelica root in water to bring down a fever. You might need to add lemon, honey, and brandy to make it more palatable.

Remedies for Fever

You can calm a fever by applying cool water compresses to the legs and feet. Add some lavender or peppermint essential oils. Remove the compresses as soon as they warm up.

To combat infection you could use a cooled infusion of rosemary instead of cool water.

Angelica root boiled and infused in water will help to bring down a fever. Add the juice of two lemons, some honey and a drop of brandy to make it more palatable. Teas and tisanes that help to check a fever include hibiscus and basil.

For those with a cast-iron stomach, treat laryngitis with a syrup made up of grated horseradish root, lemon juice, and honey which has been left to stand in hot milk or water, then strained.

Hay Fever and Asthma

Hay fever is an allergy to the pollen released by grasses, flowers, and trees in spring and summer. The pollen causes cells to release histamine, which results in streaming eyes, runny nose, sneezing, and a sore itchy throat. Allergic reactions can also be caused by house-dust mites or the fur of animals or feathers of birds. Asthma is on the increase in the Western world—the jury is still out on the cause—but many people believe pollution to be a major factor.

Remedies for Hay Fever

In the old days people chewed natural honeycomb, which was supposed to protect them from allergies of every type. You can still find it in some health stores and it is worth a try. Eating plenty of garlic is also thought to counteract allergic reactions. Chamomile tea is a natural antihistamine—add honey to build up your immunity to pollen.

Pollen brings misery to many every year in the form of hay fever, which produces itchy eyes, runny nose, and sneezing.

You could grate some horseradish and sniff it to help to clear out the sinuses as well as to stimulate breathing.

You could try taking a teaspoon of English mustard combined with a tablespoon of molasses first thing in the morning and last thing at night.

Natural honeycomb was once believed to protect people from all kinds of allergies.

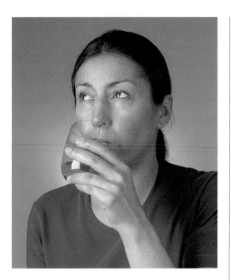

Fresh carrot juice is believed to help protect against asthma attacks. Drinking a glass a day could help to reduce the risk.

Remedies for Asthma

Nettles and onions can protect against asthma. Or try soaking a fresh cabbage leaf in hot water until saturated and drink the liquid. Chew two cloves of garlic a day or make up a drink from three heads of garlic, $2\frac{1}{2}$ cups of water, $1\frac{1}{4}$ cups of cider vinegar and a spoonful of honey. Simmer the garlic cloves in the water for a half-hour, add the vinegar and honey and simmer until it forms a syrupy consistency. Drink a sherry-glassful each day. Drink a small glass of carrot juice daily to reduce the risk of asthma attacks.

Irish moss is a jelly, which you can get from some health food stores. Combine it with half an onion, two cloves of garlic and half a cup of honey to make a syrup. It can be taken every couple of hours or as needed.

Elderflower tea or syrup drunk hot at bedtime will help keep the sniffles of hay fever at bay. Make your own syrup by mixing up elderflower heads, 2 cups of brown sugar, three lemons, and two sliced oranges. Add this to $7\frac{1}{2}$ cups of water and $\frac{1}{4}$ cup of tartaric acid. Steep it in a covered bowl for 24 hours, strain into a big pan, and bring to a boil until the sugar is dissolved. Cool, then bottle or freeze, and drink as needed.

Garlic is useful for both hay fever and asthma. Chop it and add it raw to salads. A Russian remedy recommends inhaling an infusion of two or three cloves of crushed garlic added to a basin of hot water.

Hay fever symptoms can be relieved by several natural home remedies, including elderflower tea.

Back Pain

About 80 percent of us will have some form of back pain at some time in our lives. Many people suffer in silence for years because they know there simply is no cure. Rest and warmth provide some comfort, but there is also a variety of remedies, particularly poultices, that can be applied to ease the pain—even if only temporarily. With any sort of back pain it is always best to consult a doctor.

Remedies for Lumbago

Massage is an excellent remedy for most kinds of back problem. Make up a soothing massage oil from peppermint or cilantro oil in a tablespoon of almond oil. Massage it well into the muscles of the back.

Lumbago is a rheumatic pain in the lower region of the back and can be treated with similar remedies

Lumbago is rheumatic pain in the lower region of the back.

to those given for arthritis (see page 215). Some poultices may also be helpful. Cook up whole oats, then mash them with vinegar and apply them to the painful area as hot as possible.

Boil up cabbage leaves in milk until they become like jello, spread this mixture on the affected area with a cloth, and leave it on overnight, covered with gauze held in place with plaster. This helps to release toxins from the body and, although it may not endear you to your bed partner, you will feel rested after a good night's sleep!

Shake together a cup of vinegar and turpentine and add a dessertspoon of powdered camphor and a whole egg. Keep the mixture refrigerated and use as a back rub when necessary.

Remedies for Sciatica

Sciatica is an excruciating back condition caused by pressure on the sciatic nerve which

Cabbage leaves boiled up in milk turn into a kind of jello that can be applied to the back to ease the pain of lumbago.

A cupful of Epsom salts added to a hot bath will ease the pain of sciatica, particularly if it is brought on by cold and damp. A daily supplement of seaweed extract is invaluable for back pain of any sort because of its iodine content. A tablespoon of mustard or cayenne pepper in a hot bath will ease a bad back. You can also get relief from back pain by taking a warm bath infused with nettles and by having a lot of rest in a firm bed.

Make up a camphor rub from quarter of a teaspoon each of camphor and mustard powder. Add 1¼ cups of pure turpentine and 1¼ cups of sunflower oil, mix with 1¼ cups of rubbing alcohol, and shake the ingredients together. Use it to massage an aching back or any other limbs that are seized up. Keep the area warm.

runs down the back of the leg to the knee. It is caused by pressure in the lower spine, inflammation of the nerve itself, or by back strain or injury, which may need to be seen by a back expert.

Some people swear by ivy. Take two handfuls of ivy, chop well, and mix with two handfuls of bran. Stir to a paste with 1¼ cups of water and warm over a low heat for 10 minutes. Apply to the affected area using a cloth and leave for a half-hour.

Ivy leaf is believed to make an excellent remedy for sciatica.

A tablespoon of cayenne in a hot bath will help give some relief from most back problems.

GENERAL AILMENTS
Rheumatism and Arthritis

Arthritis affects the joints and bones and can be an extremely painful and debilitating condition. Rheumatism describes the swelling, soreness, stiffness, and aching of joints and includes rheumatic fever and bursitis, a painful condition resulting from inflammation of the bursa, the fluid-filled sacs that cushion the joints.

Remedies for Rheumatism

Chiles and bell peppers are rich in capsaicin, an active chemical that desensitizes nerves and controls pain. The Mayna Jivaro tribe of Peru still apply chile fruits directly to their teeth to cure toothache, and this has prompted Western doctors to run trials to see if it may work as a pain reliever for rheumatic diseases.

Native Americans used to swear by a poultice of sage, tobacco, angelica, and balsam

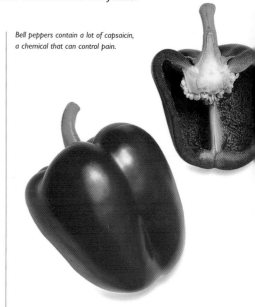

Bell peppers contain a lot of capsaicin, a chemical that can control pain.

Yogurt with grated apple and raw oats can help to reduce joint pain.

for rheumatic aches and pains. A less dramatic remedy is Epsom salts added to a hot bath, which will ease the pain, or try mixing a scant tablespoon of dried mustard or cayenne pepper into your bathwater.

Eat plenty of onions and garlic—you can even make up a delicious onion drink by chopping up three unpeeled onions and boiling them gently in 2½ cups of water.

Garlic pounded in olive oil with parsley and eaten on whole-wheat bread has been known to help, or a breakfast of grated apple with raw oats and yogurt is also good.

Remedies for Arthritis

Turmeric is a well-known cure for arthritis, so use plenty in your food. Drink warm milk with a teaspoon of ground turmeric mixed in three times a day. A back rub made from a scant tablespoon of cayenne pepper in a cup of olive oil and applied to inflamed joints will bring a soothing heat to the aching area. Boil 2½ cups of apple cider vinegar with a scant tablespoon of cayenne pepper, cool and use as a compress on the affected area. Cayenne can cause skin irritation, so make sure it heats the area but does not cause burning.

A good preventative measure is to mix a teaspoon of cider vinegar and honey in hot water and drink it first thing in the morning. Or try drinking the juice of one lemon in hot water sweetened with honey before breakfast.

Nettle soup, which is made with fresh nettle tops, chopped onion, and garlic, or plain nettle tea, are both tried and tested remedies for arthritis.

Potatoes can provide pain relief for arthritis sufferers.

Potatoes have excellent anti-inflammatory properties and can relieve pain. To make a potato poultice, boil three large potatoes in their skins until tender. Place them in some cheesecloth and mash. Apply the sack to the affected area. Remove it only after it has cooled down completely.

Remedies for Bursitis

Make a poultice of cooked cabbage leaves, mashed and applied warm between layers of gauze or cheesecloth. Linseed, marshmallow, and slippery elm are other comforting herbs that can be taken as supplements. Boil up hot apple cider vinegar with cayenne pepper and apply as a compress, as for arthritis.

Turmeric can be used in many dishes and even drunk added to warm milk to counter the pain of arthritis.

GENERAL AILMENTS
Hangovers

The best way to avoid a hangover is to avoid too much alcohol! However, that is little consolation if you are suffering the agonies of a banging head, parched throat, and the constant threat of being sick. If you know you have drunk too much, you can prevent a hangover by drinking at least 5 cups of water before going to bed. This will help to flush out some of the toxins. Colas and sodas can also help your throbbing head because they alkalize the acid in the stomach.

Remedies for Hangovers

For some reason, eggs have always been a big feature of hangover cures across all cultures. And, in fact, eggs do contain a certain chemical now known to neutralize the effects of alcohol, so it seems that the old eggnog remedy or fried eggs the morning after may work well after all!

For an upset stomach or nausea, try grating some fresh ginger root into a mug of boiling water and sipping it slowly.

Colas and sodas alkalize the acid in the stomach and help to stop the banging sensation in your head.

Tea made from fresh ginger will soothe a queasy stomach when you have drunk too much the night before.

Drinking ginger tea will also soothe your stomach, and it tastes delicious, too.

Umeboshi plums, available at Asian markets and health food stores, have long been reputed to cure hangovers. They may make some people want to vomit, but those people who have managed to keep them down swear by them.

One of the best herbal fixits for a hangover is peppermint tea. Adding organic honey will also ease your headache and begin the process of rehydration.

Replenish your lost vitamin C with a glass of fresh orange juice and add a teaspoon of lime juice or a dash of cumin powder to really get you back in gear. Drinking a cup of thyme

Eat, drink, and be merry! But be prepared for the morning after the night before and have a natural hangover remedy to hand.

tea will ease your headache and queasy stomach more effectively and safely than many over-the-counter pain relievers.

Try the hair of the dog! Peel a whole head of garlic and put in a pan with 1½ cups of red wine. Bring to a boil and simmer for 20 minutes. Strain and drink slowly. It is the tannins, not the alcohol, that help to cure your banging head!

Once you can face food again, a vegetable broth which is high in potassium and natural minerals will help to replace lost fluids and minerals. Make it from celery stalks, zucchini, beets or carrots. Try to avoid sulfur-containing vegetables such as broccoli, onions, and cabbage. Replace intestinal flora with good bacteria from live yogurt.

Try a soothing bath with essential oils of eucalyptus, peppermint, and sandalwood. A cup of peppermint tea will also help if you are feeling queasy. Soak a towel in ice-cold water and wrap it around your forehead. The coldness should help to shrink away your headache.

Cook a healthy broth using vegetables to replace lost minerals and fluids.

GENERAL AILMENTS
Stomach Troubles

Indigestion is often known as heartburn, and as its name suggests, it causes a feeling of discomfort just below the breastbone around the heart area. Eating too much, too quickly, is the main cause of indigestion, with symptoms varying from wind and rumblings in the stomach to pain or nausea.

Remedies for Indigestion

Infuse fresh mint and drink sweetened with honey for nausea.

Ripe bananas are natural antacids and can soothe an inflamed stomach. If none is available, try cider vinegar or lemon juice in hot water, which alkalizes an acid stomach. Ginger tea, made from fresh ginger root if possible, also warms and soothes an acid stomach. Drink an infusion of hot peppermint tea or try teas such as fennel, lemon balm, or cinnamon. Slippery elm powder dissolved in hot water gives immediate relief.

Mix two tablespoons of baking soda with one teaspoon of ground ginger in cold water and drink before sitting down to breakfast to prevent indigestion.

Tea made from peppermint helps combat feelings of nausea.

Remedies for Nausea

Peppermint is considered to be an excellent cure for nausea. Although it has long been associated with the relief of indigestion and travel sickness, how it works is little understood. It is believed to work by relaxing the

Water

- Avoid drinking water with a meal because it dilutes the gastric acid and leads to incomplete digestion.
- Water can also cause the fats and oils in the food to cling together, which stops them being absorbed properly.
- Drink water ten minutes before or three hours after eating.

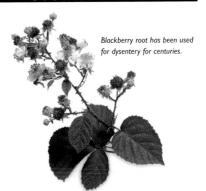

Blackberry root has been used for dysentery for centuries.

esophageal sphincter and equalizing gastric pressures. Buy readymade peppermint tea bags or put four drops of peppermint oil, found with the cookery ingredients in the grocery store, in some hot water and let it cool. Drink slowly for quick relief from nausea. Infuse some fresh mint and drink sweetened with honey.

Remedies for Food Poisoning

Food poisoning can cause terrible vomiting, diarrhea, and stomach cramps. It is the body's way of getting rid of food that is bad or disagrees with it and is usually caused by germs that inflame the lining of the stomach and intestines. The main problem

with food poisoning is fluid loss which causes dehydration, so it is important to keep up your liquid intake.

In the old days, remedies included a disgusting concoction of salt swiftly followed by a spoonful of castor oil. For mild food poisoning take raw garlic, which helps to fight the infection in the gut. Replace lost fluid by drinking plain water or diluted fruit juice.

Blackberry root has been used for years to combat the deadly form of dysentery so common in hot climates. During the American Revolution both sides accepted truces so that troops could go "rooting" for blackberry roots and leaves. It is still one of the safest remedies for children's diarrhea.

Stewed fennel, horseradish leaves, or a strong dose of apple cider vinegar have all been used to help remove bad food from the digestive system.

Ripe bananas are believed to be natural antacids. They can provide relief from inflammation of the stomach.

Cystitis and Bladder Conditions

Cystitis is a painful condition caused by inflammation of the bladder. Symptoms include pain in the lower back and a stabbing pain when urinating. It is important to seek your doctor's advice if you have cystitis for any length of time, because if it continues, it can lead to kidney infection. Cystitis has been called the "honeymoon disease" because it often occurs after sex. Drinking water and urinating as soon after sex as possible may help to prevent an attack.

Remedies for Cystitis

Plain water flushes out the kidneys better than anything and will help to get rid of the bacteria that are causing the infection. Drink plenty and often. Make up 2¼ cups of mild chamomile tea and drink it throughout the day to flush germs out of the bladder.

Try one teaspoon of baking soda in a glass of tepid water every three hours. It makes the urine less acidic, which stops bacteria from breeding—it also relieves the burning sensation that so often accompanies cystitis.

Apply live yogurt to the affected area—its friendly bacteria can help to fight invading germs. Make up some homemade barley water by boiling up a cupful of barley in enough water to cover it. Add the zest of a lemon and simmer until the barley is soft. Strain off the barley, add some honey, and sip slowly throughout the day.

Plain live yogurt is a traditional natural home remedy used to combat the discomfort of cystitis.

Cranberry juice can reach the parts that other juices can't reach. A substance in cranberries appears to prevent bacteria from sticking to the walls of the urinary tract where they would normally proliferate. When you drink cranberry juice, the bacteria lose their grip and are washed away.

Cranberry juice is a well-known cure for cystitis.

Make an onion soup from three or four onions steeped in 4¼ cups of hot water. Drink it throughout the day—it tastes disgusting but does the trick. Horseradish also stimulates digestion and encourages the kidneys to flush through urine. Horseradish can be grated into foods or boiled up with mustard seed and water as a drink.

Experts now believe the same component may also be present in blueberries. Eat the berries or pulp them with a little water in a food processor.

Turnips, celery stalk, fennel, and onions are all good diuretics; so are dandelion roots and stinging nettle leaves. Add any of these raw to salads.

Onions are a good diuretic, and can be added to many different dishes, including soups and salads.

Kidney beans, soya beans, and black-eye peas can make an appetizing dish which really benefits the kidneys.

Kidney beans are also helpful for any kidney or urinary tract infections. You can also try black soybeans or black-eye peas. Cook them with garlic and use them to replace meat in the diet. Chinese herbalists swear by seaweed, fenugreek, and saw palmetto for good results.

GENERAL AILMENTS
Bowel Problems

Constipation, diarrhea, irritable bowel syndrome (IBS), and piles are four of the most debilitating conditions known to humankind—made all the worse because nobody wants to talk about them. Constipation occurs for many reasons, the most common of which is poor bowel habits learned from a young age, and can lead to piles. Medications including antidepressants can also cause constipation. Diarrhea is often the result of food poisoning, and either constipation or diarrhea can be symptoms of IBS.

Remedies for Constipation

Anyone who remembers syrup of figs from their childhood will not be at all surprised to learn that both figs and prunes are well-known laxatives.

Figs and prunes are effective laxatives and can help to ease the discomfort of constipation.

laxative effect and are particularly useful when constipation is due to excessive meat or fat in the diet.

Drinking cooked cabbage or carrot juice can also help to ease constipation, or you could mash up raw apricots with a little honey in a bowl of yogurt.

Rhubarb stewed with honey will also have the desired effect. Strawberries have a mild

Strawberries have a mildly laxative effect and so can help with constipation.

Remedies for Diarrhea

Rice pudding is one of the oldest remedies for diarrhea. Make your own with one and a half cups of milk, a pinch of salt, six tablespoons of brown sugar, a teaspoon of vanilla extract, two to four eggs, grated lemon rind, and two cups of cooked white rice. Add all the ingredients together and mix well. Spread the mixture in a buttered baking dish and cook for an hour. Sprinkle with cinnamon.

Boil rice in water for one and a half hours, then strain and drink the liquid to soothe an

Try grated apple that has gone brown—the oxidized pectin acts like an over-the-counter medicine to cure diarrhea.

irritated bowel. You could also make a thick oatmeal drink by cooking together a cup of oats and 2 pints (1.2 liters) of water for five minutes. Strain and drink frequently. Oats also have a calming effect on the bowel, and starchy fluids tend to stop vomiting and reduce fluid loss.

Add a teaspoon of cornstarch to a glass of water at room temperature—it tastes disgusting, so drink it down quickly and repeat the dose every three or four hours.

Blueberries contain compounds called anthocyanosides which control diarrhea, so add them to your breakfast cereal.

Try eating a grated apple which has been allowed to go brown. The pectin oxidizes and acts like many proprietary brands of diarrhea remedies—slightly unripe bananas have the same effect.

Remedies for IBS

Peppermint has a well proven anti-spasmodic effect on the smooth muscle of the intestines—drink peppermint tea or, if you have mint growing in your garden, chew the

fresh leaves or sprinkle them on salads. Potatoes can reduce stomach acid as they contain small amounts of atropine which has an antispasmodic effect. Wash and dice a large potato and steep it overnight in a cup of cold water with salt. Strain and drink the water every morning on an empty stomach. A two-day diet of potatoes will flush out toxins and waste from the body and help to purify the blood.

Remedy for Piles

Rub a small amount of either witch hazel or lemon juice into the affected area with a cotton wool swab before going to bed.

Rice pudding is one of the oldest remedies for diarrhea.

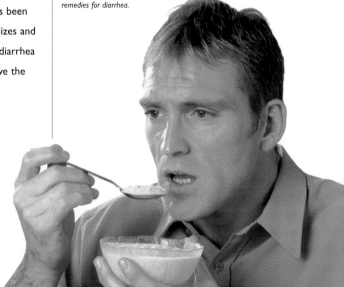

Skin Problems

Skin problems often reflect what is happening inside the body. Acne normally appears at adolescence and is believed to be caused by hormonal imbalances which produce too much of the oily substance in the skin known as sebum. Psoriasis occurs when skin cells reproduce up to a hundred times faster than normal. The skin then builds up in dry, flaky patches and causes itching and irritation.

Remedies for Acne

Avocado may be rich in fatty oils but it also contains plenty of vitamins A, C, E, and B complex, which are all essential for good skin. It has strong antibacterial and antifungal properties, so it is excellent for acne or any other irritating skin conditions. Make up a paste of avocado pulp and apply to any dry skin rashes to soothe and moisturise.

Grate some horseradish, which is rich in sulfur, and infuse it in hot milk for a half hour. Strain it and use the liquid as a face wash. You can also

Avocados contain all the vitamins – A, B complex, C and E – needed for a healthy skin.

leave a teaspoon of the grated root to dissolve in a cupful of cider vinegar for a week and use it in the same way. It will sting badly but works a treat.

Remedies for Eczema

Make a paste from a teaspoon of powdered marshmallow root or slippery elm mixed with hot water. Spread it onto the affected area and leave for 20 minutes, then wash off with an infusion of comfrey. Comfrey leaves also make a wonderful facial wash and will promote growth of new tissue.

Make a rice-flour poultice and apply it hot to the affected area. Eat plenty of asparagus, which helps promote the elimination of toxins through urine and is also considered a liver

Eating a grapefruit a day is a routine that can help relieve the symptoms of psoriasis.

Comfrey leaves can be turned into a great facial wash for those affected by eczema.

tonic because of its high amino acid content. Drink the water of the asparagus after it has been steamed.

Beets were used by the Romans to relieve fever, but they also stimulate the immune system and help to clear the blood. Drink the juice of cabbage, which contains antibacterial properties, to promote healing, and eat plenty of watercress, which contains sulfur.

Dandelions are a fantastic detoxifier of the liver, kidneys, blood, and tissues. Use a tincture of dandelion roots for eczema or acne.

Remedies for Psoriasis

Make up an antifungal herbal tea from hops. Eat a grapefruit a day for breakfast. Drink cranberry juice, eat prunes and plums, and avoid alcohol and smoking.

Make up a dandelion wine from a bunch of dandelion petals, 9 pints (5 liters) of water, two oranges and two lemons, cut into pieces, a pinch of yeast, and 3 pounds (1.3kg) of sugar. Boil the dandelion petals for 20 minutes and pour over the orange and lemon pieces. Allow the mixture to cool, then add the yeast and let it stand for 48 hours. Strain the mixture through cheesecloth and pour into a pitcher. Let the wine stand for around six weeks before bottling. Keep for at least six months before drinking.

Eating plenty of watercress, which contains sulfur, is recommended as a treatment for eczema.

Toothache and Gum Disease

Unfortunately, toothache is an all-too-familiar condition in the Western world, and it is usually the result of poor care of the teeth and gums. Halitosis (bad breath) is often caused by sore gums or abscesses in the mouth.

Remedies for Toothache

Oil of cloves or a dried clove rubbed onto the gum around an aching tooth will help soothe it. Try chewing a clove over the offending tooth for instant relief, or pack dried hops or fresh peppermint into the tooth.

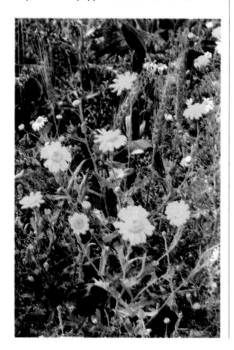

Raw cloves rubbed onto the offending tooth can cure a toothache, or chew one whole to find instant relief.

In Germany, dentists use a clove-based anesthetic to eradicate the pain of toothache. Native Americans used to apply the mashed green leaves or root of the willow as a poultice for toothache. You could make a mouthwash of vinegar and salt to ease the pain. Apply ground black pepper and fresh ginger to a piece of gauze and pack the tooth with it.

If you are not worried about being antisocial, you could plug a cavity with cotton wool soaked in onion or garlic juice. It will disinfect the whole area and give some relief from the pain.

You could try putting a slice of lightly boiled apple between the teeth to help to relieve the pain of toothache.

You can make a tincture of marigold that will help to ease the pain of a bad tooth or sore gums.

Remedies for Sore Gums

Cabbage is known for its anti-inflammatory properties, so you could dab a little white cabbage juice onto mouth sores.

Sore gums may be the result of vitamin B and C deficiency, so strengthen your gums by drinking plenty of rose hip or blackcurrant tea and tisanes.

Soak a small pad of cotton wool in tincture of marigold and press it to the sore gum or bad tooth.

Make a mouthwash out of marigold or agrimony, boiled in water and left to cool.

A tincture of lavender leaves rubbed onto the gums acts as an excellent antiseptic, or you could gargle with a cooled infusion of lavender leaves mixed with honey.

You can make your own natural toothpowder by mixing two parts of baking of soda to one part salt. If you have none to hand, you could even try cleaning your teeth with raw lemon.

Tincture of lavender leaves rubbed on the gum acts as an antiseptic.

Blueberries are astringent and antiseptic and are therefore good for combating mouth ulcers and gum infection.

Remedies for Mouth Ulcers

Eat plenty of blueberries—they are astringent and act as a strong antiseptic, and so they can be useful for mouth ulcers or sores and infections of the gums.

Try mixing two teaspoons of sea salt and two teaspoons of hydrogen peroxide in a large glass of warm water as a mouthwash. (NB: Don't swallow.) Hot salt water held in the mouth over an abscess also helps to disperse it.

Mouth Fresheners

- Try chewing on a few sprigs of parsley to freshen the mouth.
- Crush cloves in a cupful of boiling water, cool for five minutes, and then use as a mouthwash.

Migraine and Headache

Most people experience headaches at some time or another. Some are caused by tension or stress; others are the result of too much alcohol or may herald a cold or flu. Migraine is more than just a serious headache. It is actually a neurological disorder which includes a pounding headache along with visual disturbance, nausea, and vomiting. If you have a headache that persists for any length of time, see a doctor.

Remedies for Headache

A warm cabbage leaf compress placed on the head can help to ease a headache, or try eating a crust of stale brown bread with butter and marmalade—a curious remedy, but very effective! A poultice of cucumber or raw potatoes placed on the brow can relieve a headache caused by too much sun.

Lavender will help to refresh and clear your head. You can make up your own

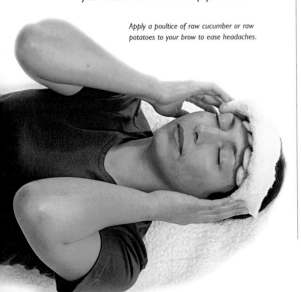

Apply a poultice of raw cucumber or raw potatoes to your brow to ease headaches.

Steam inhalation is the best cure for a sinus headache. You can add various essential oils to help increase its efficacy.

lavender water with two tablespoons of dried lavender, two teaspoons of cinnamon, a pinch of grated nutmeg, and 4¼ cups of surgical spirit. Breathe in the delicious fumes for instant relief. Headaches caused by hypertension can also be eased by eating garlic, which lowers blood pressure.

Remedies for Sinus Headache

The herb feverfew has been proven in clinical trials to have an effect on migraine.

Sinus headaches respond best to steam inhalations. Add the essential oils of pine, eucalyptus, rosemary, or thyme, either on their own or in combination. Apply a hot compress of plain water to the forehead. You can also infuse the water with lavender or peppermint oils. Lie down and breathe in the aroma, keeping the compress hot.

Remedies for Migraine

Feverfew is the main herb proven to have an effect on migraine. Oregano has also been reported to be effective—the dried leaf can be used as snuff to clear a blocked head, or simmer the fresh leaf in olive oil and use it to massage the temples.

A drink made from fresh ginger root has been shown to be almost as effective at preventing migraines (when taken daily) as powerful prescription drugs.

Add ginger oil to almond oil and massage onto the temples during early warning signs. Or try soaking your feet in a footbath which has either fresh ginger or peppermint added, or their essential oil. The bath will draw the blood away from the head to the heat and provide some relief.

Eating a bowl of canned tomatoes simmered with basil and served with a dash of vinegar has been known to help migraine. Make up an ointment out of oregano oil and petroleum jelly and smooth onto the temples.

If you can get hold of feverfew, make up a tea from the herb. If not, try peppermint and rosemary. Use two parts peppermint leaves and one part rosemary and let them steep in a mug of hot water for at least ten minutes.

A crust of stale brown bread spread with butter and marmalade seems to work for headaches.

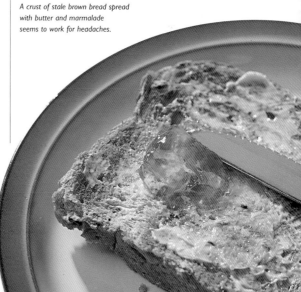

GENERAL AILMENTS

Earache and Neuralgia

Earache can be caused by a variety of things, from colds and catarrh to enlarged adenoids or an infection of the inner ear. Most home remedies are based on warmth and oil, but you should never poke the ear, no matter how bad the pain.

Any inflammation of the trigeminal nerve, which carries sensations into the skull near the ear, produces an excruciating spasmodic pain in one side of the face known as neuralgia. At one time, grated horseradish would have been applied to the cheek until the pain subsided, but nowadays there are less harsh ways of curing the condition.

A hot water bottle wrapped in an old sweater can help soothe earache or neuralgia.

A lump of salt rolled in a hot, damp cloth and held against the ear can relieve earache.

Remedies for Earache

Many earaches result from colds, flu, or other types of congestion. If this is the case, you can reduce the mucus and phlegm with a tea made from elderflowers or a cold elderberry drink.

One of the best remedies for earache is a hot water bottle covered in a warm sweater and held close to the ear. Put a few drops of warm olive oil in the ear and lie on the opposite side for about five minutes while the oil flows down into the inner ear.

Crush a clove of garlic and let it rest in some warm olive oil for fifteen minutes, then strain the liquid. Soak a cotton wool ball in the liquid and place it just inside the outer earlobe.

Garlic, crushed and soaked in olive oil, can be an effective means of countering infection in the ear.

Remedies for Neuralgia

Massage the gums right at the back of the mouth with a clove. Sleeping with a hop pillow has been known to cure this most painful of conditions, or try holding a hot poultice of porridge oats wrapped in cheesecloth against the area. Eating oats can also act as a stress reducer and excellent pain reliever.

The garlic combats infection. In the old days, a boiled onion placed on the affected ear was supposed to be a marvelous cure. Some used the juice of the onion in a warm oil.

You could also heat a teaspoon of almond oil and pour gently into the ear, then plug with a piece of cotton wool.

As a compress, try a lump of salt rolled in a cloth, steeped in hot water and wrung out, or a baked potato wrapped in wool—use both remedies as hot as you can stand it for the best effect.

Drink plantain tea to tone up the delicate membranes of the inner ear and prevent dizziness from ear inflammations.

A hop pillow could provide just the solution you need for relief from painful neuralgia.

Olive oil, warmed and dropped into the ear, will provide relief from pain.

Period Pains and PMS

Period pains, also known as dysmenorrhea, are the searing pains felt in the lower abdomen by more than half the female population during a period. About 15 percent of those women say the pain interferes with their everyday lives. Period pains tend to start during adolescence and become less severe with age—particularly after having a baby.

Cramp-like pains in the lower abdomen at the start of a period are rarely a sign of illness but can cause great misery. Premenstrual syndrome (PMS) affects about 40 percent of women and causes severe mood swings, headaches, bloating, and sore breasts.

Remedies for Period Pains

Brown rice, wholemeal bread, oats, nuts, and beans will all increase the magnesium, iron,

Oats and brown rice help to fight period pains.

Massage warm castor oil over the lower abdomen to help to ease period pains and relieve the bloating of PMS.

zinc, and vitamins in your body, which help you to fight pain. A warm bath with a few drops of chamomile or clary sage essential oils will ease tension and relax muscles. Geranium and rosemary essential oils counter fluid retention.

Angelica is a warming, stimulating herb suitable for women who feel a chill during periods. To make a tea, add one part each of angelica, chamomile, and ginger root to 2½ cups of water and simmer for 15 minutes.

Dandelion is a good source of iron and is one of the best diuretics, supplying plenty of potassium which helps to get rid of excess water. Add young dandelion leaves to a fresh green salad for an appetizing remedy. Yarrow tea can help ease menstrual cramps and decrease menstrual bleeding.

Massage warm castor oil over the lower abdomen. Hot, fresh ginger tea or fresh ginger infused in milk is one of the oldest remedies for period pains. Boil up rhubarb roots into a tea, or try basil tea if you suffer with cramps and particularly heavy periods.

Remedies for PMS

Peppermint tea can help to ease the symptoms of PMS. Freshly cooked asparagus helps to control breast tenderness and bloating. Seaweed may also help—it's the natural iodine that relieves symptoms. Choose wakame, nori, and kombu, and use them in stews or soups.

Seaweed contains natural iodine that is useful in relieving PMS symptoms. Edible seaweed is available for use in stews and soups.

A castor oil poultice placed on the lower abdomen will encourage the clearing of toxins through the lymphatic system. Soak an old hand towel in castor oil and place it over the abdomen, cover it with another towel, and place a hot water bottle on top.

Dandelion tea can help with bloating in the run-up to a period. It rids the body of excess fluids. Sage tea also helps, or you can eat either in a leaf salad. Make up a cocktail of spinach, watercress, young nettle shoots, carrots, and beets. Use the raw ingredients in a juicer if you have one, or cook the carrots and beets and process everything in a blender. This combination acts as a wonderful tonic at this time of the month.

Freshly cooked asparagus helps to alleviate the symptoms of breast tenderness and bloating associated with PMS.

Hot Flushes and Menopausal Problems

Hot flushes, night sweats, and mood swings are all symptoms of the menopause, which, although not an illness, can cause untold misery to many women as they get older. Cutting out caffeine is particularly useful for most symptoms of menopause, and there is a range of teas and tisanes which can actively help to relieve symptoms.

Remedies for Hot Flushes

Mint is a famous cooler, so add fresh mint whenever you can to salads. Drink peppermint tea or add some peppermint essential oil to your bathwater.

Sage leaves can be made into a tonic wine that helps to relieve hot flushes.

Sage is known to be the herb of old age. Make up a sage tonic wine by taking a handful of fresh sage leaves and letting them stand in a bottle of good quality white wine for at least two weeks. Sweeten with honey and leave for another week. Strain the liquid through a cloth and bottle it. Drinking a glass before lunch and dinner is most beneficial.

Another great menopause tonic contains borage leaf, lemon balm, raspberry leaf, burdock root, and plantain leaf. All you need to do is to steep the herbs in hot water and drink the liquid during the day in order to lift your spirits.

Celery stalk contains estrogen-stimulating substances that will help with menopausal symptoms.

Pumpkin seeds contain phytoestrogens, which can help with menopausal symptoms.

Remedies for Night Sweats

Drink two cupfuls of sage tea each day. Place three teaspoons of sage leaves in a pan and pour two cups of boiling water over them. Cover and simmer for five minutes. Make it up in the morning and keep it in a thermos for drinking during the day. Ginseng tea is often recommended because it contains plenty of B vitamins and minerals. It also helps boost a flagging libido!

Try marigold tea made from an infusion of flower heads in 4¼ cups of boiling water, steeped for ten minutes. Drink it three or four times a day.

Place the leaves of lemon balm under your pillow at night, or drink a cup of lemon balm tea to soothe and revive you.

Remedies for General Symptoms

Calendula, hops, ginseng, sage, and wild yam all have estrogenic action which can be helpful—take these as an infusion or supplement. Eat plenty of rhubarb, oats, and celery stalks which contain similar estrogen-stimulating substances.

Some foods have high levels of phytoestrogens (natural plant estrogens), and these may have a beneficial effect on menopausal symptoms.

Many of these compounds, which are called isoflavones and lignans, are found in soy foods, flax seeds, and some herbs.

In Asia, where women eat a diet high in soy foods, they report fewer menopausal symptoms and also have a lower incidence of breast cancer. Some trials have also shown that a diet high in soy decreases the incidence of hot flushes.

Other foods that contain phytoestrogens include mung beans, pumpkin seeds, tofu, and tempeh, so try to include these foods in your diet.

Eat plenty of nettles, dandelion, and plantain, which can all be added to salads.

As a general tonic, you could run yourself a hot bath and add essential oils of rosemary or lavender, and this will soothe and refresh you.

Lemon balm leaves, placed under your pillow at night, will soothe you and help you to counter night sweats.

Candida/Thrush

Stress, allergies, too much junk food, and alcohol can all conspire to cause an imbalance in the flora of the gut, colon, or vagina, causing the itching and soreness known as candida or thrush. Thrush is a fungal parasite, which can be stimulated by the contraceptive pill or by the use of antibiotics. Simple self-help includes avoiding synthetic underwear or tight jeans and avoiding sex while you have the infection. Oral thrush is more common in babies and children than in adults, and it can be caused by too much sugar in the diet.

Remedies for Vaginal Thrush

Thyme, in the form of a tea, can be used as a douche to ease the discomfort of thrush.

Eat a pot of live yogurt every morning or make up a breakfast of raw oats, live yogurt, and orange juice. A weak solution of one teaspoon of hydrogen peroxide in a glass of warm water, dabbed gently onto the affected area with a swab of cotton wool, will ease the itching.

Live yogurt contains friendly bacteria known as acidophilus, which combat vaginal yeast and other infections caused by this fungus. Put some on a tampon and insert into the vagina (remove within two hours).

Drink honey in cider vinegar each morning, and if you are on a course of antibiotics, eat as much raw garlic as you can take for up to a week—it counters most bacterial, fungal, and viral infections. You can even place a peeled clove of garlic wrapped in a little gauze inside the vagina for a powerful local antiseptic effect—it stings like mad, so this one is not for the faint-hearted!

Live yogurt contains friendly bacteria which combat vaginal yeast.

Fresh coconut and coconut milk are good for combating the symptoms of thrush.

solution. Leave the tampon in for four to five hours once or twice a week.

Nasturtium is an age-old remedy for thrush because the flowers act as a natural antibiotic. You could make an infusion from the flowers and use it in a cool bath.

Remedies for Oral Thrush

The best remedies for oral thrush include eating plenty of garlic and lots of live yogurt. Rinse the mouth thoroughly with a solution of apple cider vinegar and warm water with a dash of salt.

Some other foods, such as onions, coconut, and coconut milk, are also thought to be particularly helpful against thrush.

You could make up a douche from 2½ cups of boiled, cooled water to which you have added two drops of lavender oil, or make a douche from chamomile or thyme tea. You can also use either of these mixtures in a shallow bath to ease the discomfort.

Use myrrh or tea tree oil diluted with a teaspoon of vodka and soak a tampon in the

The flowers of the nasturtium act as a natural antibiotic. Use them in an infusion or in a cool bath.

Chilblains, Cramp, and Poor Circulation

Chilblains are a mild form of frostbite and are painful, itchy swellings that generally occur on the hands, feet, or ears in response to cold weather. They are usually the result of poor circulation, which can in turn be aggravated by smoking. Some naturopaths believe that cramps and poor circulation are also caused by low potassium or calcium levels.   ●

Remedies for Chilblains

Whatever you do, resist the urge to put your feet on a radiator or a hot water bottle. Get the circulation going by rubbing the feet briskly with a towel.

As long as the skin is not cut or cracked, dust cayenne powder on the chilblains to stimulate blood circulation. If the skin is broken, rub in calendula ointment to promote healing.

One method is to chop up 1 pound of turnips in their skins. Boil in 12 cups of water till soft. Soak the affected part in the water while it is still hot but bearable, rubbing pieces of turnip over the inflamed surfaces. The salts and essential oils present in the turnip act as an astringent while also improving the circulation.

Celery stalk contains compounds that lower blood pressure and help to improve circulation.

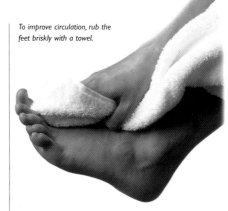

To improve circulation, rub the feet briskly with a towel.

Try fresh horseradish root, bandaged into place. Lemon, garlic, or onion juice rubbed on the chilblains can be very effective, or bandage a piece of pithy lemon zest, garlic, or onion in place overnight.

Celery stalk is also a good remedy for chilblains. Simmer a bunch of stalks in 4¼ cups of water for an hour and soak your feet in a bowl of the mixture for an hour. Make it as hot as you can stand it and try it first thing in the morning and before going to bed.

Remedies for Cramp

Celery stalk contains compounds that reduce high blood pressure by relaxing the smooth muscle lining the blood vessels. The blood flows more freely and pressure drops; this helps cramp symptoms.

Mix one tablespoon of apple cider vinegar and one teaspoon of honey in a glass of warm water. Gulp it down quickly and the discomfort will disappear after only a few minutes.

Much potassium may be lost in many of the commercial brands of vinegar now available, so look out for the unprocessed variety in a health store.

How to Make a Calcium Supplement

- Fill a jar halfway with crushed eggshells.
- Cover with vinegar and allow to sit for two weeks.
- Strain, then take one to three tablespoons daily.
- You can use it as salad dressing or in sauces.
- Sweetened with honey, it can be taken as a refreshing drink.

Almonds in the diet will help to reduce the incidence of cramp.

Drink teas that are rich in calcium such as dandelion, raspberry, and plantain leaf. Eat plenty of almonds, sesame seeds, yogurt, and most green vegetables.

"Restless legs" is cramp that causes pain and twitching in the legs. Add seed oils, avocados, and wheatgerm to the diet to alleviate these symptoms. Reduce your meat, high-fat dairy produce, and salt intake.

Soak your feet in a solution made from boiled celery stalks to ease chilblains.

Eye Conditions

The eye is an incredibly delicate organ and yet it has been built to withstand a large amount of punishment. The anterior part of the eyeball is encased in a tough membrane called the cornea, which can survive and recover from even quite severe injuries. However, alcohol, smoky atmospheres, and working too long at computer screens all conspire to harm, often resulting in sore, itchy or inflamed eyes.

Remedies for Tired Eyes

Rose petals can soothe inflamed or irritated eyelids.

Rose petals are a traditional remedy for inflamed or irritated eyelids. Make up a cooling and soothing compress from two or three petals steeped in a glassful of boiling water for ten minutes. Soak some cotton wool or eyepads in the cooled and strained liquid and place over the eyelids.

Chamomile or marigold tea, used cold as a compress, can also be very healing. Witch hazel, ice-cold from the refrigerator, is very refreshing when your eyes feel tired or you have been staring at a computer all day. Eat plenty of fennel, another marvelous food for tired eyes, or drink it as a tea.

Try an eyebath of three teaspoons of honey diluted in two cups of boiling water and left to cool. Or try a poultice of cabbage leaves, softened but not cooked in boiling water. You may look ridiculous with the leaves over your eyelids but it really works. A raw potato or cucumber placed over closed eyelids can have the same effect.

Borage was valued by the ancient Greeks for strengthening weak eyes and preventing cataracts. You are more likely to develop cataracts if your diet is lacking in beta-carotene, folic acid, and vitamin C. Borage contains all three, so it is a good idea to try to incorporate it in your diet.

Include plenty of fennel in your diet; it is marvelous for tired eyes.

Remedies for Styes

An eyebath of warm boracic lotion or
a poultice of fresh, steamed cabbage leaves
will disperse a stye. Or try a drop each of
the essential oils of lavender and lemon with
a teaspoon of cooled boiled water and bathe
the eye with the solution. This will also ease
the symptoms of conjunctivitis.

*World War II pilots were encouraged to eat plenty of carrots
to improve their night vision.*

Past Beliefs

Carrots were once believed to be a super-
food for eyes, and pilots during World
War II were officially encouraged
to eat plenty. In the old days, anything
golden was reputed to be benefit
the sight, including gazing
at marigolds during
the day.

Insomnia

In these stressful times it is hardly any wonder that many people find it hard to get to sleep at night. However, there are certain things you can do to promote a good night's sleep. Try to relax before going to bed, and avoid coffee and alcohol, which tend to keep you awake rather than promote good sleep. Take a warm bath with Epsom salts or play some quiet music. Have a bedtime ritual, so your brain learns to slow down before you settle down to sleep.

Remedies for Insomnia

Natives of certain parts of Italy reputedly slept with cloves of garlic between their toes to ensure a good night's sleep! The Victorians, on the other hand, favored washing the head with dill or placing dill on the pillow at night.

Adding two teaspoons of apple cider vinegar and two teaspoons of honey to a glass of hot water and drinking it at bedtime may seem a little more user-friendly. Try placing a few drops of lavender oil on the pulse points of the wrist and forehead before you go to bed—it

Eating plenty of lettuce will help you get a good night's sleep.

has a soothing and calming effect. Place celery seeds in a piece of cheesecloth and inhale the fumes as you settle down for the night.

Lettuce is supposed to contain sleep-inducing compounds, so eat it raw or drink a lettuce infusion. Mandarin oranges also have

To help combat insomnia, place some drops of lavender oil on the wrists and forehead before settling down for the night.

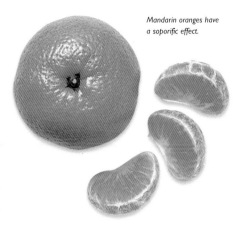

Mandarin oranges have a soporific effect.

Make up your own version with the juice of two oranges in a little hot water sweetened with honey.

A footbath is a good way to bring on sleep because it encourages the blood to flow from the head to the feet. Mix up some lavender and rosemary essential oils and add to a bowl of warm water. A mustard footbath can work just as well.

Warm milk and honey sprinkled with a pinch of cinnamon helps prepare children for sleep.

a soporific effect—it is a good idea to eat one after your evening meal.

You could make up a tea from elderberry flowers, which are thought to relax the nerves and induce sleep.

Native Americans used to eat raw onions to get a good night's sleep. They also made a sleep potion from poppy heads infused in hot water. If this seems a little drastic, try valerian tea just before going to bed.

Make up this infusion: put the ground seeds from one cardamom pod, two drops of peppermint oil, one teaspoon of sugar, and a pinch of baking soda in a cup of boiling water and drink while it is still hot.

Add a teaspoon of honey to a cup of warm milk and sprinkle with cinnamon: this is a good drink for helping wakeful children go to sleep.

Orange flower water was a traditional cure for insomnia among English gentlewomen.

Foot and Hand Care

We have no respect for our feet—we cram them into badly fitting shoes, encase them in synthetic fabrics, and demand they perform their task tirelessly, supporting us for hours on end. No wonder we suffer from all sorts of foot complaints, from bunions, calluses, and corns to unpleasant fungal infections such as athlete's foot. Although we are kinder to our hands, we still think nothing of dipping them in and out of hot water all day, which can result in chapped skin or dry nails.

Remedies for Sore Feet

For smelly feet, steep six tea bags in a large bowl of hot water, allow it to cool, and plunge your tired feet in it for ten minutes. You can also rejuvenate tired feet by soaking them for a half hour in a bowl of barley or millet mixed with hot water and cooled. Make a soothing footbath by

Oil of thyme with olive oil massaged between the toes can help heal athlete's foot.

We need to have more respect for our poor old feet! Give them a soothing footbath or massage them with essential oils as a treat.

adding one tablespoon of sea salt to a basin of warm water. In cold weather add a teaspoon of mustard powder to warm them up.

Remedies for Corns

Rub corns with castor oil daily for two weeks to get rid of them completely. Put a piece of lemon zest or raw tomato over the corn and cover with a bandage. The juice of the fruit will soften the corn overnight. The same can be done by soaking leeks in water or vinegar for 24 hours and then applying as a poultice. Make a soothing footbath by adding four or five drops of peppermint oil to a bowl of tepid water. You can also use a couple of peppermint tea bags infused for ten minutes.

Remedies for Athlete's Foot

Make up a mixture of equal parts vinegar and warm water or surgical spirit and bathe the feet in a bowl. Massage between the toes with natural yogurt, leaving it to soak in overnight. Add a few drops of essential oil of thyme or rosemary to some olive oil and massage the feet carefully between the toes.

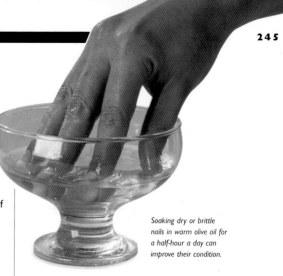

Soaking dry or brittle nails in warm olive oil for a half-hour a day can improve their condition.

Remedies for Verrucas and Warts

Peel the skin of a potato as thinly as possible. Rub the inner side of the skin on the wart twice a day. Thanks to a chemical in the potato near the skin, the wart should turn black and drop off within a couple of weeks.

The milky juice squeezed from the stem of a dandelion or celandine can also be used as a balm. Smooth it onto the affected area and cover with a plaster. The next morning the wart or verruca should have disappeared.

Remedy for Dry Hands

Mix together $1/4$ cup of ground almonds, a beaten egg, a handful of comfrey root, and a tablespoon of honey. Coat your hands with the mixture, pull on an old pair of leather or cotton gloves and wear overnight. Rinse your hands in the morning and repeat this for a week. Your hands will feel very soft and supple.

Remedies for Brittle and Stained Nails

Immerse dry or brittle nails in warm olive oil for 30 minutes a day until you see an improvement.

To remove stains, rub the hands and nails with the pithy side of a piece of lemon zest, leave for a minute and then wash off.

A mixture of ground almonds, egg, comfrey, and honey may be just the moisturizer your hands need.

S h a m p o o s ,   " F e e l   G o o d "
T r e a t m e n t s ,   a n d   T o n i c s

We tend to forget that many natural beauty treatments have been used through the ages for all sorts of cleansing creams and lotions. Cleopatra was reputed to have used aloe vera as a moisturizer, and today most proprietary brands of moisturizing cream contain this substance. Almond oil is another great skin softener—you can add whatever essential oil you feel appropriate to smoothe and pamper your skin. The condition of your hair and scalp can be affected by your general state of health, so almost any stressful condition will cause your skin and hair to appear lifeless and dull. A balanced diet is the basis of good health, hair, and skin, but here are some extra tips to give nature a helping hand!

Pamper yourself with a natural, homemade shampoo or "feel good" treatment and improve your general sense of wellbeing.

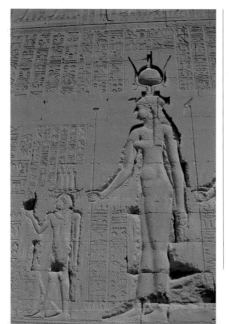

R e m e d i e s   f o r   D r y   H a i r

To keep your hair in top condition, try massaging a few drops of oil of rosemary into the scalp, then rinsing with an infusion of nettles. For very dry hair, warm two tablespoons of olive oil in a cup placed in a pan of hot water. Massage the oil into the scalp. Steep a towel in hot water, wring it out and wrap it around your head for about two

Even the ancient Egyptians needed a little help to stay beautiful! Cleopatra was reputed to have used aloe vera as a moisturizer.

hours. Rinse with a solution of half a cupful of cider vinegar to 11 cups of water.

Make an egg shampoo for dry hair. Use 1 tablespoon of fresh rosemary, 2½ cups of hot water and one egg. Steep the rosemary in the water for 20 minutes and allow to cool. Beat in the egg. Massage into the hair and rinse well.

Remedies for Dandruff

Cut a lemon in half and rub the two halves into the scalp. Leave for ten minutes, then wash the hair. Sour milk has the same effect but will not smell as nice.

Wrap one or two pieces of fresh ginger root in cheesecloth. Boil it up in 2½ cups of water. After shampooing, rinse your hair with the liquid, massaging it into the hair.

Rinse your hair with cider vinegar, wrap your head in a towel and leave for a half hour. Rinse out completely. Repeat three times a week until the dandruff disappears.

Remedy for Split Ends

Comb in a mixture of equal quantities of warmed castor oil and olive oil. Follow this by shampooing with an egg yolk. Wrap your head up in a warm towel and let the egg yolk soak in for at least an hour.

Aloe vera has been used in moisturizers through the ages and is still used today.

Then add half a cup of cider vinegar to 20 cups of cool water and rinse the mixture through your hair, followed by a cool rinse with clear water to remove all traces. For thinning hair, rinse your hair with flat beer.

"Feel Good" Tonics

Make yourself a natural tonic. Some people swear by drinking a teaspoon of apple cider vinegar and a teaspoon of honey in ¾–1 cup of hot water mid-morning and mid-afternoon. It provides a boost of energy which carries them through to the next meal.

Or try making up a purifying tonic by mixing a tablespoon of crushed blueberries and a tablespoon of shredded watercress with 1¼ cups of boiling water poured over. Cover the liquid and leave to cool, then strain it. Drink a cup twice a day. It's guaranteed to make you feel a million dollars.

You can make an egg shampoo with rosemary—it works wonders for dry hair problems.

Green grapes can be used in a homemade facial cleanser.

For a dandelion tonic, pick enough dandelion flower heads to make 5 cups of petals. Cut off the stem and collar at the end of each flower. Rinse the dandelions in water before preparing the petals. Place the petals in a pan, cover with 11 cups of water, and boil for 20 minutes. Add two oranges and two lemons. Add a spoonful of baker's yeast and allow to stand for 48 hours before straining through cheesecloth. Add 3 pounds of sugar and stir well. Use as a feel good tonic whenever you need one.

For the Face

You can make a natural cleansing cream with eight tablespoons of beeswax heated up with 2 cups of liquid paraffin. Add 1¼ cups of water to the wax and oil mixture, stirring continuously. Leave it to cool and transfer it to jars for storage.

To make a cleanser, mix ten green grapes, two teaspoons of apple cider vinegar, one teaspoon of honey, and a teaspoon of oatmeal in a blender until the liquid becomes sticky. Clean your face and neck in your usual way and apply the mixture, leaving it on for at least five minutes. Rinse with warm water and pat dry.

Lemons are marvelous for greasy skin that is prone to blackheads—you can drink the juice and also apply it to the skin. Its high antioxidant content makes it an excellent treatment for wrinkles too. Dilute it with mineral water and massage it gently at the first sign of wrinkles, particularly around the mouth and eyes.

To make a face pack for greasy skin, pit and mash a large cucumber, add a teaspoon of lemon juice, a teaspoon of witch hazel, an egg white, and two tablespoons of cream or plain yogurt, and blend all the ingredients in a blender. Apply the mixture to the face and leave for 20 to 30 minutes until nearly dry, then rinse well with warm water.

For a great face mask, mix an equal

Make up a face pack for greasy skin from natural ingredients such as cucumber.

Kelp added to bathwater will help to improve circulation and reduce cellulite.

quantity of oatmeal and ground almonds into a paste by adding enough liquid to thicken the mixture and smooth onto the face and neck. Add one teaspoon of wheatgerm or brewer's yeast for dry skin, or kaolin to draw out spots and impurities.

If you have problem skin, Fuller's earth (a clay available at drug stores) will help an oily skin and stimulate the blood supply. Witch hazel, beaten egg white, yogurt, or lemon juice will all help to dry up an oily skin. Egg yolk, honey, soured cream, pulped bananas, or avocado will all benefit a dry skin. Rosemary oil added to a base of oats and almonds will invigorate a tired, dull-looking skin.

You could use the pulp of the pawpaw fruit to rub over the face and this will help to slough off dead skin cells.

A tablespoon of castor oil mixed with two tablespoons of almond oil makes an excellent eye make-up remover.

For Cellulite

Cellulite is the term used to describe the puckered areas of fatty flesh, often referred to as "orange peel skin," that generally occur around the tops of the thighs, hips, buttocks, and upper arms, and is more common in women than men. No one really knows what causes cellulite, yet theories abound on how it can be treated.

Fresh parsley is a rich source of vitamin C, a good detoxifier, and a diuretic, so it helps the body eliminate excess water. Eat plenty of the raw herb in salads.

Boil up the zest of a lemon in water and leave it overnight. You then drink it first thing in the morning.

Use kelp in your bathwater—it boosts the circulation. Dandelion tea will rid the body of any excess fluid.

Chop two handfuls of ivy leaves and mix with four handfuls of bran and enough warm water to make a paste. This can then be applied to the affected areas as a poultice.

The pulp of the pawpaw fruit will slough off dead skin cells.

Useful Home Remedies

Almond oil: as a base for massage and rubs; for earache

Aloe vera: as a facial cleanser

Angelica: use the leaves or roots as a diuretic, expectorant, antispasmodic; digestive tonic for children's coughs and colds; for fainting fits; for a fever

Asparagus: for eczema

Avocado: as a hand cream; as a cleanser; for sunburn; for cuts and grazes; for acne

Baking soda: for sunburn; for cystitis

Bananas: for diarrhea

Barley: for cystitis

Basil: as an antiseptic

Beets: for fever; to clear the blood; for acne

Blackberry leaves: for diarrhea; for food poisoning

Blackcurrants: for infection and inflammation

Blueberries: for cystitis; for diarrhea; for mouth ulcers and sore gums

Borage: for coughs; for constipation; as a diuretic

Buttermilk: for sunburn

Cabbage: for arthritis and rheumatism; as a poultice for back pain; as a detoxifier; for asthma; for constipation

Camphor oil: stimulant or sedative; antiseptic, can be used on cuts and grazes; for lumbago

Carrots: for stomach disorders; for cleansing the system; for eye problems; for asthma; for constipation

Castor oil: for food poisoning

Cayenne pepper: as a poultice for joint irritation; with garlic for a bad sore throat

Celandine: for jaundice, throat infections, verrucas and warts, failing eyesight

Celery: for urinary tract infections

Chile peppers: for rheumatism

Cider vinegar: can be used for practically anything. It cures fungal infections, stomach infections and can be used in a footbath for athlete's foot

Cinnamon: a warming digestive, antispasmodic and antiseptic; good for menstrual cramps and for diarrhea; with ginger for a chesty cough

Cloves: as a painkiller for toothache and to ease wasp stings; can also help nausea; for a fever

Comfrey: for bruises and sprains

Cowslip: contains salicin (like aspirin)

Cranberries: the perfect answer to cystitis

Cream: for wounds

Cucumber: with glycerine for burns; for headaches

Dandelion: a diuretic and can be used to cleanse the whole system of toxins; good for mosquito bites

Dock leaves: for nettle stings

Echinacea: an antibiotic; for colds and flu

Egg yolk: for a gravel graze; for a hangover; for lumbago

Elderberries: for burns and sunburn; for coughs; for earache; for fever; for headaches; for insomnia; for toothaches; for neuralgia

Epsom salts: for back pain; for infections; for menstrual pain

Fennel: for bad breath; for indigestion; for constipation; for colds and flu; as a diuretic

Feverfew: for migraine

Figs: for constipation

Friar's balsam: as an inhalant for allergies, e.g. asthma and hay fever; for cuts and grazes

Fuller's earth: clay for use as a face pack to draw impurities from the skin

Garlic: as a natural antibiotic and antiseptic; for cleaning wounds; for stomach disorders; for cleansing the blood; for corns; for coughs; for earache; for diarrhea; for hangovers; for thrush; for verrucas; as an insect repellent

Ginger: for arthritis and rheumatism; for colds and circulation problems; in a footbath for headaches and migraine

Grapefruit: for psoriasis

Hibiscus: for a fever

Honey: for asthma and allergies; for constipation; for coughs, colds and fever; for sore throats; for cuts and grazes

Honeycomb: chewed for allergies

Hops: for insomnia; for headaches

Horseradish: for acne; for chilblains; for mosquito bites; for sinuses

Hyssop: in tea to support the iimmune system

Irish moss: for asthma

Ivy: for cellulite; for sciatica

Lavender: for acne; for burns; for coughs and colds; for earache; for a hangover; in a hair treatment; for menstrual cramps; for rheumatism; for the skin; for thrush; for sprains

Lemon: for colds; as a digestive; for fever; in hair and skin treatments; for teeth; for stings

Lemon balm: for burns

Lemon juice: for sunburn; for bites and stings

Linseed: in a poultice for bursitis

Marigold: for bruises and burns; for sore gums

Marshmallow: for bursitis; for eczema

Milk: in rice pudding for diarrhea; with cinnamon for insomnia

Milk of magnesia: for indigestion; for sunburn

Mud and clay: for sunburn

Mustard: as a rub for bad backs; in a footbath for colds or flu

Nettles: as a diuretic; for cleansing the blood; for eliminating toxins; in soup for insomnia

Oats: for stress; for cleansing the blood; in a poultice for cellulite; for menopause and period pains

Olive oil: for food poisoning

Onions: for colds; for cystitis; to help digestion; for allergies

Oregano: for migraine

Parsley: for bad breath; as a diuretic

Pepper: for toothache

Peppermint: for nausea; for colds and fever; for headache; for menopause; as a mosquito repellent; for IBS

Plums: for psoriasis

Potato: for stomach disorders; for sore eyes; as an anti-inflammatory; for IBS

Prunes: for constipation; for psoriasis

Rice: for bowel disorders, especially diarrhea

Rosemary: as a disinfectant; for fever; for headaches; in hair treatments; as a mouthwash; for rheumatism

Rose petals: as an eye treatment

Sage: for thrush; for menopause; for mouth/gums; for sore throats

Salt: as a gargle for sore throats; for fungal infections; in water for cuts and grazes

Sandalwood: in a bath for a hangover

Slippery elm: for indigestion; for bursitis

Soya: for menopausal symptoms

Strawberries: as a laxative for constipation

Thyme: for colds; as a disinfectant in a footbath; as an infusion for improving a hoarse voice

Tomatoes (canned): for migraine

Turmeric: for sprains; for rheumatism

Turnips: for coughs and colds; (boiled) for cystitis

Umeboshi plums: for food poisoning; for hangovers

Watercress: for acne

Willow: for toothache

Wine: for hangovers; garlic wine as a tonic

Witch hazel: first-line treatment for cuts and grazes; as a deodorant; for hemorrhoids

Yogurt: for cuts and grazes; for thrush

Index

acne 224
Aconite 24, 64
acute conditions 13
addictions 28, 52
Afghanistan 158, 163, 167
Africa 149, 164, 169, 171
ailments 206–243
allergies 210–211
amber 137, 144, 150, 182, 185
amethyst 132, 137, 164, 182–183, 187
angelica 84
antiseptics 196
Apis mel. 25, 64
aquamarine 135, 137, 159, 187
Argent. nit. 15, 26
Arnica 27, 63, 64
aromatherapy 70-71, 73, 74, 77, 80–81
Arsen. alb. 16, 28
arthritis 215
asthma 79, 211
athlete's foot 245
Atlas cedarwood 72, 87
Aurum met. 29
Australia 157, 161, 168, 173, 175, 179
autumn blend 121

babies 79
back pain 212–213
bathing 78, 79, 80
bathrooms 183
baths 194
bedrooms 123, 182
bee stings 200
Belladonna 30
bergamot 78, 116
berries 106–111
beryl 137
birthstones 187
bites 200–201
black pepper 107
bladder conditions 25, 34, 220–221
blends, essential oil 81, 119, 120–21
blood pressure 79, 196–197
blues blend 121
body 143, 181
bowel problems 222–223
Brazil 137, 151–153, 156, 161,
     164–169, 171–172, 179
breastfeeding 78
British Crown Jewels 138–139, 162
brittle nails 245
bruises 27, 204–205
Bryonia 31
Burma (see also Myanmar) 138
burns 198
bursitis 215

buying crystals 186–187
buying oils 124–125

Calc. carb. 16, 32
Calc. phos. 33
calcium supplement 239
Calendula 63, 65
camphor 77
candida 60, 236–237
Cantharis 34, 64
Carbo veg. 35
cardamom 74, 108
carnelian 137, 151, 183, 187
carrier oils 78, 81, 118–120
cars 123
cedarwood 72, 87
celestite 160, 182
cellulite 249
chakras 142–145, 181
chalcedony 137, 151
Chamomilla 36
chapped skin 199
chest relief blend 120
chilblains 238
children 79, 123, 124
China (country) 138, 155
China (remedy) 37
cholesterol 194
chronic conditions 13
citrine 152, 183
citrus 73, 74–75, 77, 78–79, 125
cleansing crystals 137, 146–147
cleansing, facial 118–119, 248–249
clinical trials 194–195
Coffea 38
coffee 23
colds 194, 197, 206–207
collecting crystals 187
color healing 142–145
combination skin 118–119
compresses 195
computers 172, 182
constipation 222
constitutional remedies 13, 14–22
coriander 111
corns 244
correspondences 144
corundum 137
coughs 24, 39, 40, 53, 207
cramp 196, 239
creams 63
crust, Earth's 134–135
Crystal Palace 139
Cullinan diamond 139, 168
cultivation 75
cuts 48, 202–203

cypress 93
cystitis 25, 34, 220–221

dandruff 247
diagnosis 9
diamond 132, 137, 139–141, 168, 187
diarrhea 222–223
diet 23
digestive problems 49
dilution 11
dining room 122
disinfectants 196
distillation 75, 76
doctors 8–9
dosage 13
double terminations 136
dowsing 181
Drosera 39
drugs 194–196
dry
     hair 246–247
     hands 245
     nails 245

emerald 135, 137, 138,
     140–141, 156
emotions 14, 45, 51
enfleurage 76
epilepsy 79
essential oils 23, 68–129, 183, 195
eucalyptus 77, 80, 96
exhaustion 35, 37, 46, 57, 62
expiry dates 23
expression 75
extraction methods 75, 136–137
eye problems 25, 59, 240–241

face treatments 118–119, 248–249
faces 136
fainting 205
fears 14
feel-good treatments 246–249
fevers 209
field dressings 197
first-aid 198–205
first-aid kit 64–65
flavorings 77
flowers 70, 73, 78, 100–105
flu 40, 206–207
food 77
food poisoning 219
foot blend 120
foot care 244–245
fractures 35, 58
frankincense 73, 88
frequencies, crystal 146

frequency of treatment 13
fruits 73, 78, 112–117

garnet 132, 137, 144, 149, 187
Gelsemium 40, 64
general ailments 206–243
geography 74–75
geranium 74, 101
ginger 82
glands 143
glossaries 126–127, 188–189
gold 176
grapefruit 78, 115
grapeseed 78, 81, 120
Graphites 17, 41, 63, 65
grazes 48, 202–203
Guatemala 155
gum disease 50, 227

Hahnemann, Samuel 10
hair care 246–247
Hamamelis 42, 63
hand care 244–245
hangovers 52, 216–217
Hawaii 154
hay fever 210–211
headaches 24–27, 29, 31–32, 45,
    47, 58, 228–229
healing methods 180–181
health food stores 9, 12
heart disease 29
hematite 179
Hepar sulph. 43
high blood pressure 79, 196–197
Hippocrates 10
history, home remedies 196–197
Hollywood 140
home remedies
    first-aid 198–205
    general ailments 206–243
    hand and foot care 244–245
    history 196–197
    treatments and tonics 246–249
    useful home remedies 250–253
home use, essential oils 122–123
homeopaths 9, 10
hot flushes 234
Hypericum 44, 65, 63
Ignatia 17, 45
igneous rock 135
inclusions 136
India 132, 138–139, 143, 149, 151,
    161, 165, 166, 168, 173, 183
indigestion 218
inflammation 30, 196
influenza 40, 206–207

infusions 195
inhalation 79, 80, 194, 195
insomnia 38, 242–243
Internet 9
iolite 165
irritable bowel syndrome (IBS) 223

jade 138, 155
jasmine 73, 74, 75
jellyfish stings 201
jewelry 132–133, 138–139, 142
jojoba 81, 118–119, 120
juniper 73, 110

Kali phos. 46
Kent, James T. 10
kitchens 122
Koh–i–noor 139
Kunz, George 167
kunzite 167

labradorite 137, 144, 174
Lachesis 18, 47
lactating 78
lapis lazuli 138, 163, 187
lavender 73, 74–75, 78–79, 80, 100
leaves 73, 90–99
Ledum 48, 65
lemon 74, 78, 81, 113
lemongrass 98
lime 78, 117
living rooms 122, 183
localized modalities 23
lumbago 212
Lycopodium 18, 49

Madagascar 152, 156, 160, 161,
    165–167, 171
mail order 9
mandarin 74, 78, 114
marjoram 74, 90
massage 78–79, 81, 120–121
massage balms 63
mature skin 79, 118–119
may chang 109
Maya 138
meditation 133, 144, 181, 184–185
menopause 47, 57, 234–235
mental factors 14
Merc. sol. 19, 50
metamorphic rock 135
migraine 195, 229
mimosa 73
minerals 134–135, 136–137, 141
mining 136–138
mint 23

modalities 14, 23
moisturising 119
moldavite 157
mood mixtures 121
moonstone 132, 137, 161, 187
mosquito bites 200–201
mother tincture 11
mouth fresheners 227
mouth ulcers 50, 227
movies 141
Mozambique 159, 165
muscle rubs 195
muscle tone blend 120
muscular problems 55, 56
Myanmar 138, 148, 155, 162, 165, 173
myrrh 73, 89

nails 245
Namibia 164
National Health Service (NHS) 9
Native Americans 144, 170
native elements 137
Natrum mur. 19, 51
nausea 196, 218–219
neck blend 120
neroli 79, 105
nerve problems 53
neuralgia 231
New Age 141
night sweats 235
normal skin 118–119, 248–249
nutmeg 106
Nux vomica 20, 52, 65

obsidian 170
offices 182–183
oily skin 118–119, 248–249
ointments 63
opal 137, 175, 187
oral thrush 60, 237
oral use, essential oils 77, 78
orange 73, 74, 78–79, 94, 105, 112
organic minerals 137
oxides 137
Pakistan 156, 159, 171
palmarosa 99
patchouli 74, 95
pearl 137
pendulums 180–181
peppermint 77, 91
perfumes 23, 70, 76
peridot 138, 154, 182, 187
period pains 232–233
Persia 158
personality traits 10
personality types 10, 14–22

petitgrain 94
pharmaceuticals 77
pharmacies 9, 12
Phosphorus 20, 53
phototoxic oils 78–79
physical factors 15, 23
physical tonics 120
piles 223
pillules 12
planes 123
plants 70–73, 76
PMT blend 121
potentization 11
poultices 195
powders 12–13
pregnancy 78
premenstrual syndrome (PMS) 32, 121, 233
programing crystals 147
proving 10
psoriasis 225
Pulsatilla 21, 54
pyrite 137, 177

quartz 132, 134–137, 146, 169, 184–185
quinine 10

remedies, homeopathic 23–62
resin oils 88–89
rheumatism 214–215
Rhus tox. 55, 63, 65
rock types 135
roman chamomile 79, 104
roots 72, 82–85
rose 73, 75, 79, 103
rose quartz 137, 166, 181, 182–183
rosemary 74–75, 79, 92
ruby 135, 148
Russia 164, 168, 174, 177
Ruta grav. 56, 63

safety 77, 78–79, 124
sandalwood 72, 74, 79, 80, 86
sapphire 135, 140, 162
scalds 198
sciatica 212–213
seasonal affective disorder (SAD) 19, 29
seasonal treats 121
sedimentary rock 135
seeds 73, 106–111
self–treatment 8–9, 11
sensitive skin 118–119
Sepia 21, 57
shampoos 246–247
shelf life 124–125
shock 205

shoulder blend 120
Sicily 135, 160
side effects 11, 194
silicates 137
Silicea 22, 58
silver 178
sinus headaches 229
skin
  dry 118–119, 199, 245
  problems 43, 44, 224–225
  sensitive reactions 78–79, 81, 125
  see also eczema
skincare 118–119, 248–249
smoking 23
smoky quartz 137, 172, 182
soft tablets 12
solvent extraction 75
sore
  feet 244
  gums 50, 227
  throats 24, 30, 34, 40, 58, 194, 208–209
Sotheby's 140
South Africa 137, 149, 168, 173, 177
South America 138, 151–156, 164
split ends 247
sprains 204–205
sprays 63
spring blend 121
Sri Lanka 137, 138, 149, 161, 162, 165, 171
St. Edward's Crown 138
Staphysagria 59
steam distillation 75
steam inhalation 195
stinging nettles 201
stings 200–201
storage 23, 124–125
stress 47
studies (offices) 182–183
styes 59, 241
succussion 11
sulphides 137
Sulfur 22, 60
summer blend 121
sunburn 199
Superman 141
suppliers 9, 12, 77, 124–125, 186
swallowing 77, 78, 124
sweet almond 78–79, 81, 119, 120
tablets 12
tea tree 74–75, 78, 80–81, 97
teas 195
temperament 14
temperature 23
terminations 136, 146
thrush 60, 236–237
Thuja 61, 63

Tiffany & Co. 167
tiger's eye 137, 173, 182–183
time (modality) 23
tinctures 63, 195
tired eyes 240
tonics 120–121, 246–247
toning 119
toothache 226
toothpaste 23
topaz 153, 187
topical applications 63
tourmaline 137, 171, 187
Tower of London 138
trains 123
travel 123
travel kit 64–65
travel sickness 218
treatment tips, homeopathic 24–62
tropical blend 121
tuberose 73
tummy troubles 194, 218–219
turmeric 72, 85
turquoise 158, 187

USA 149, 157, 159–160, 166–172, 174–178

vaginal thrush 60, 236–237
vaporization 79, 81
varicose veins 42, 47
Venus' hair 136
verrucas 61, 245
vetiver 72, 74–75, 83
visualization 181, 187

warts 61, 245
wasp stings 200
water 203, 219, 220
websites 66–67, 128–129, 190–191
winter blend 121
wood 72–73, 86–87
wounds 48, 197, 202–203

ylang ylang 79, 102
yoga 143

Zambia 156, 159, 164
Zinc. met. 62